TRANS FORM

UNSTUDIO

Lars Müller Publishers

CONTENTS

PREFACE 4
POSITIVE NOTE A 10
POSITIVE NOTE B 12

1 A CAPACITY FOR ENDLESSNESS 17

2 THE STRUCTURE OF MOVEMENT 103

3 BLOB TO BOX 151

4 V-MODEL 193

5 CROSSING POINTS 213

6 BIG DETAIL 251

PROJECT CREDITS 312

PREFACE

In these rapidly changing times, we increasingly embrace change and innovation. In all facets of our lives, we deviate, modify, shift and pivot to challenge and disrupt long accepted norms. Transformation has also always been a central facet of the architectural profession, the built environment and of our work at UNStudio.

Back in the 1980s, when the controlled chaos of the Deconstructivists emerged on the architectural scene, their opposition to the ordered rationality of Modernism and

Postmodernism brought about an anarchic disruption to the status quo and demonstrated that new thoughts about architecture could always be generated. But whilst the Deconstructivists were the first architects to eschew architectural history and the eclectic model of the Post-modernists, many of us felt at the time that their idea of removing functionalism from being a priority led to the creation of a randomness in architecture that did not reflect our own position.

For us, architecture was not principally about creating form.

We believed in an architecture that could provide powerful new experiences. At UNStudio, such experiences are derived from conceptual models and theoretical ideas transforming to become physical, tactile and functional. As such, we set about developing architectural systems from such models; integrated systems where the experience, geometry and functionality of the building merge and become fully synthesised.

At UNStudio we have always believed in enriching the future through constant transformation. Compiling this book has given us an opportunity to rethink the cultural edge and conceptual thinking that has formed the basis of our designs for over 30 years. In it, we attempt to illustrate our creative process and demonstrate how theoretical ideas and conceptual models are developed by our practice into physical form.

In the end, the following pages serve to illustrate that, as a creative endeavour, architecture ultimately always lands somewhere between art and airports.

Ben van Berkel

This book can be transformed into a glowing object.

The top and side of this
book have been printed
with a phosphorescent ink.

The ink will be most effective
in complete darkness.

In order to give light it must catch light.

Phosphorescence is
a special case of luminescence,
whereby absorbed light is
emitted again. This effect is also
referred to as 'Glow in the dark'
or 'After-glow'.

This ink is totally free of hazardous radioactive substances.

POSITIVE NOTE A

Thank God architecture is not art. Do architects kill themselves, cut off body parts, and imbibe dramatic quantities of dangerous substances? On the whole not. Architecture suffers less from self-imposed restrictions and instructions than the fine arts. Of course architects labour under the same yoke as anyone else; architects too must seek to produce work that is original, innovative, reflective and relevant to all that seems to be original, innovative, reflective and relevant in the present time but that continuous mirror effect does not have the same crushing effect as it has on art. Because outside the frame of the artistic looking glass the architect faces the client, and engages with questions of utility, sustainability, economy, and construction. The fact that the architectural search for form is invested with so many questions and demands makes it easy. Architecture today is the lighter art; fine art has become a bit heavy since it has been pronounced dead so often.

POSITIVE NOTE B

Thank God that architecture is art. Or is halfway art, being, so to speak, located between art and airports. The airport, or rather, the network of airports, is the most extreme example of architecture as the accumulation of late-Capitalist logistics; the air-port is a portal, a business, a science fiction fantasy, an escalation of short-lived consumption, a non-place, a unique system which has some of the characteristics of the city, but also a high-risk disaster site, a place where incredible densities of people collect, and a place where we experience strong emotions such as fear, loss, and elation. Well, the relation between architecture and the airport is obvious. But how about art? Today, poetic notions of the ideal city are useless in view of the highly specific, public, relational systems that work within a global economy. Taking a new look at the convergence of spatial and socio-economic structures raises specific questions, such as: what are the spatial and structural characteristics of our intensified late-Capitalist systems of production and consumption? How can we envisage these systems to change the living and working environment, while protecting the environment? We need to develop a specifically architectural perspective on those new types of urban conditions, using information from sociological, economic, geographical and human-itarian sources as well as ways of seeing inherent in the architectural discipline itself. But even as we collect, manipulate and present information, we realize the insufficiency of our diligent, and hopefully imaginative, tracing of movement patterns, user groups, and the various virtual and infrastructural ways in which we distribute ourselves over the earth. For what does it all mean? These numbers tell us too little about the motives triggering all these patterns, or about the effects of these structures and constellations. We end up sculpting the statistics, painting with information in bold brutal brushstrokes or refined minimalist gestures, just like any old artist.

1 A Capacity for Endlessness

ARNHEM CENTRAL STATION TERMINAL ROOF

Arnhem (NL)

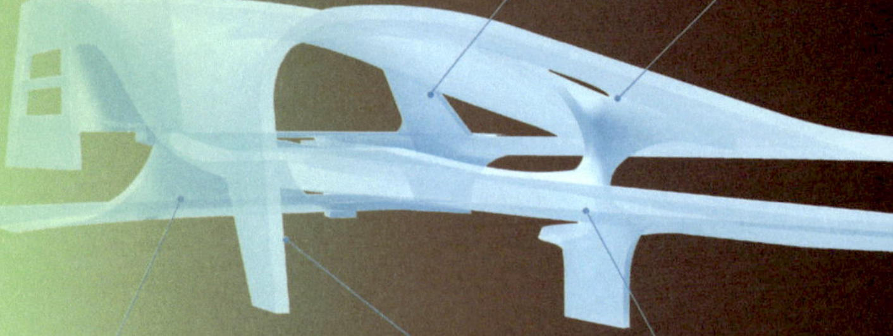
back twist
twist
flip
V-wall
balcony

09_03-11
Area=4.01m²
delta-z=69.36mm
10_03-11
Area=3.34m²
delta-z=3.34mm
10_02-11
Area=4.1m²
delta-z=18.83mm
10_01-11
Area=4.08m²
delta-z=15.51mm
10_02-10
Area=4.02m²
delta-z=9.34mm
10_01-10
Area=4.06m²
delta-z=20.79mm
11_01-08
Area=3.72m²
delta-z=61.65mm

D
Arnhem
E

C
B
A

MERCEDES-BENZ MUSEUM
Stuttgart (DE)

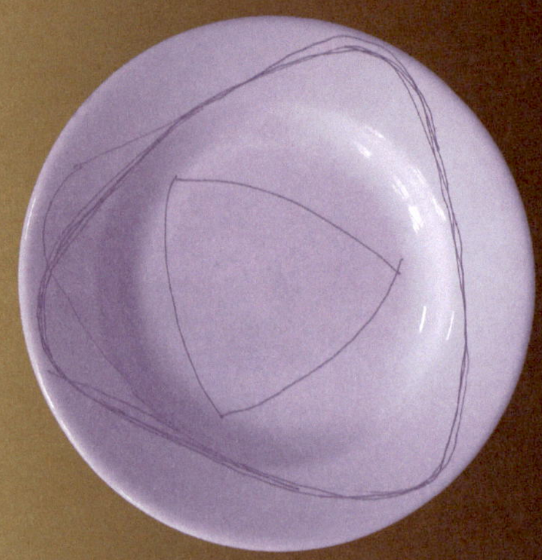

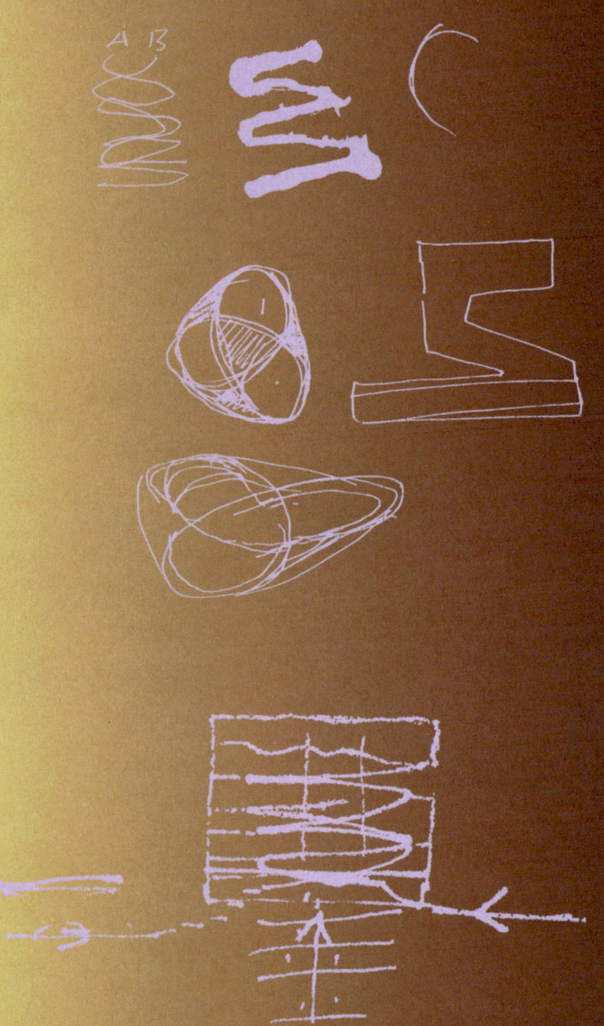
A B

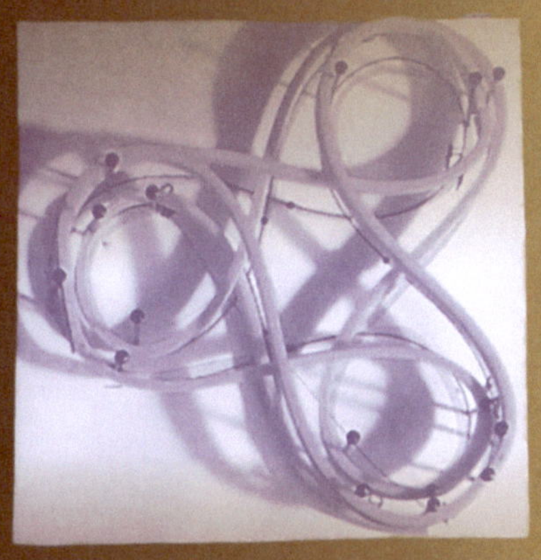

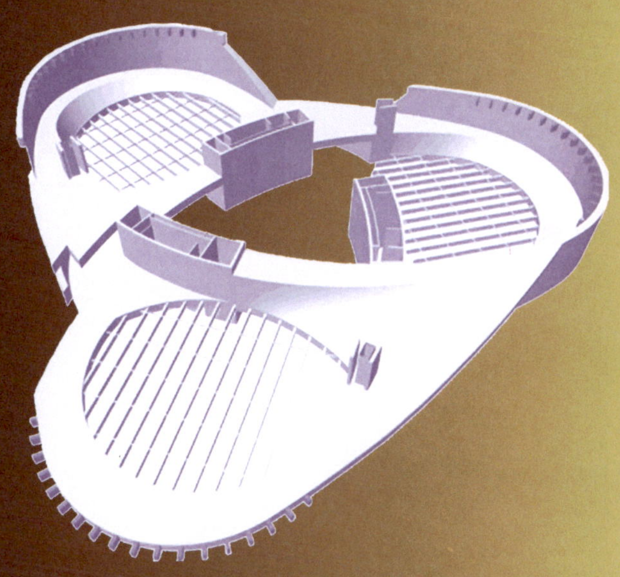

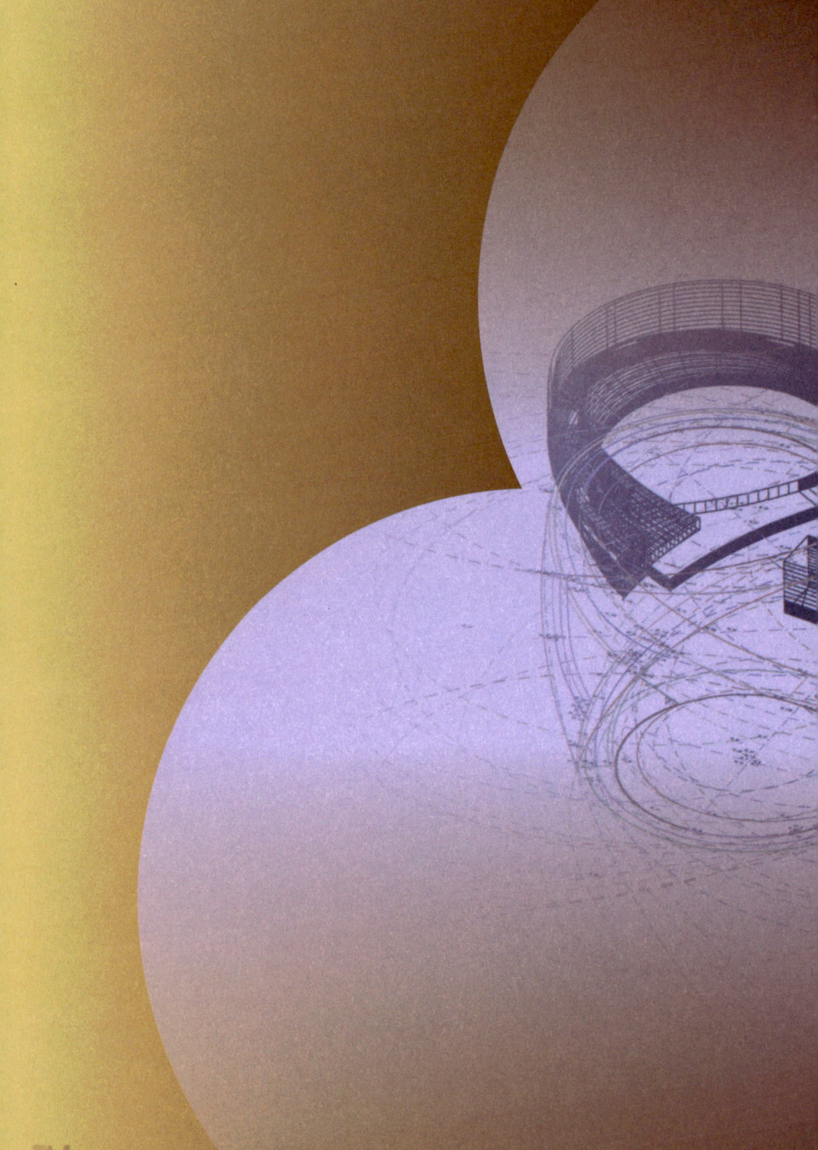

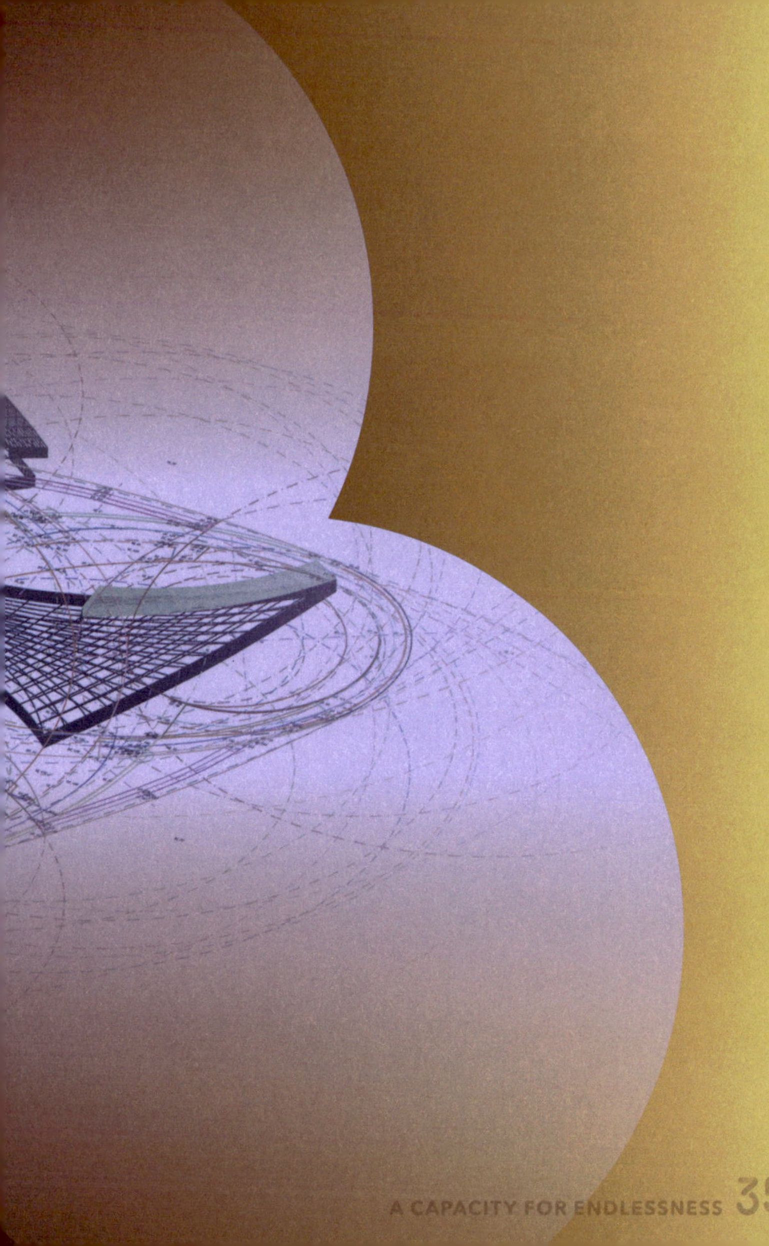

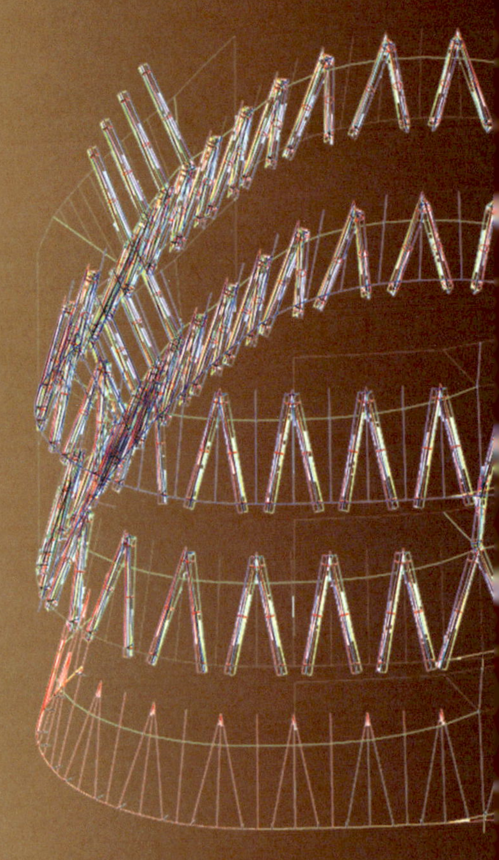

ZÜBLIN
WM

Mercedes-Benz Museum

LIVING TOMORROW

Amsterdam (NL)

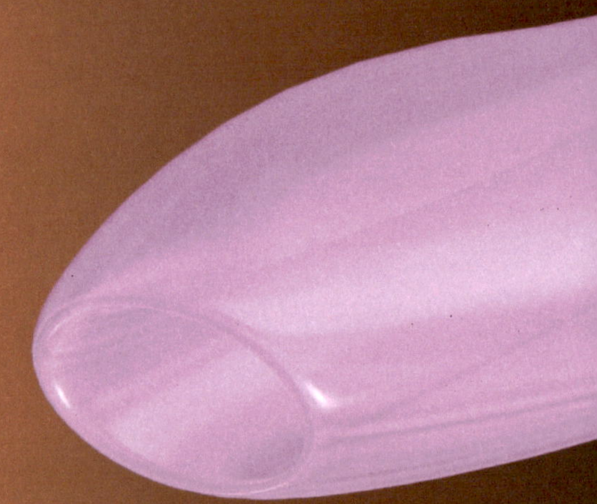

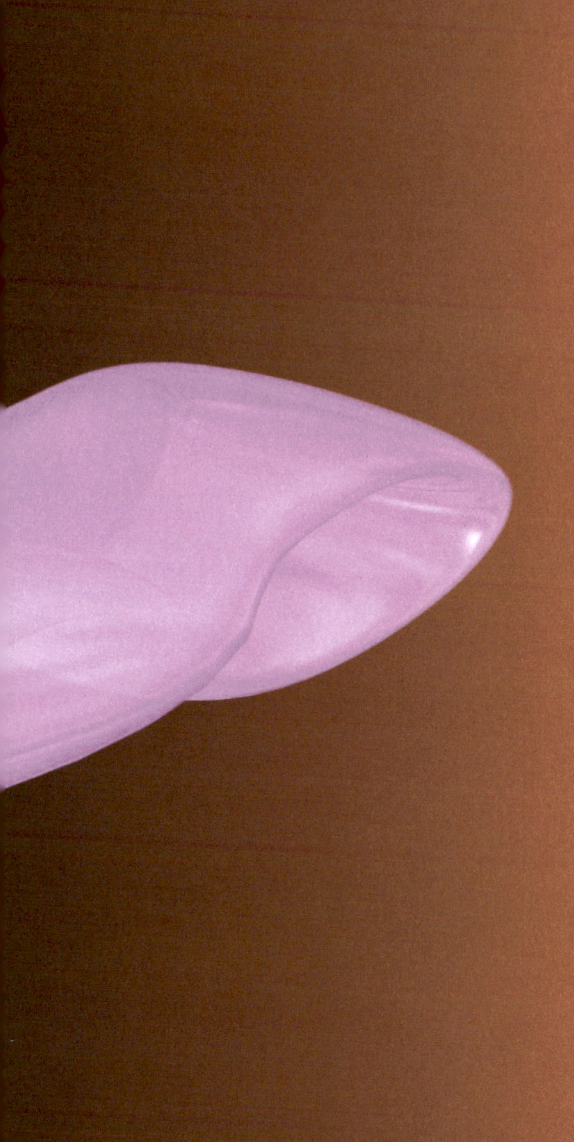

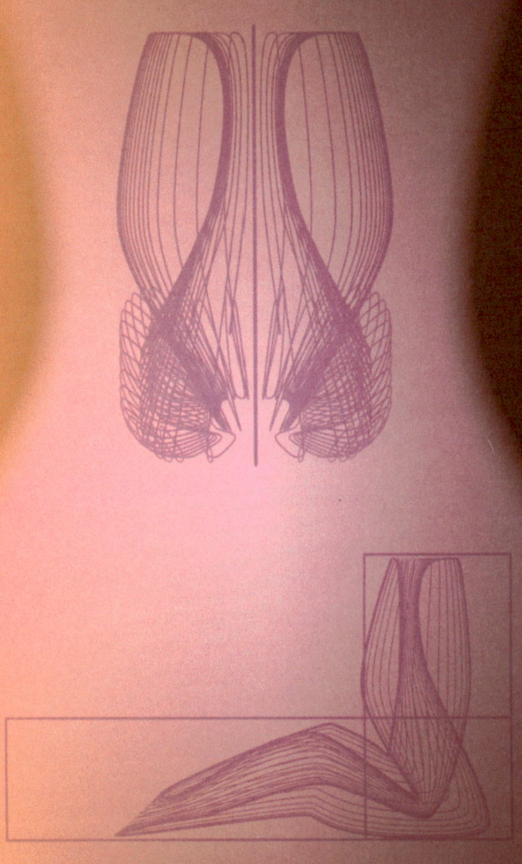

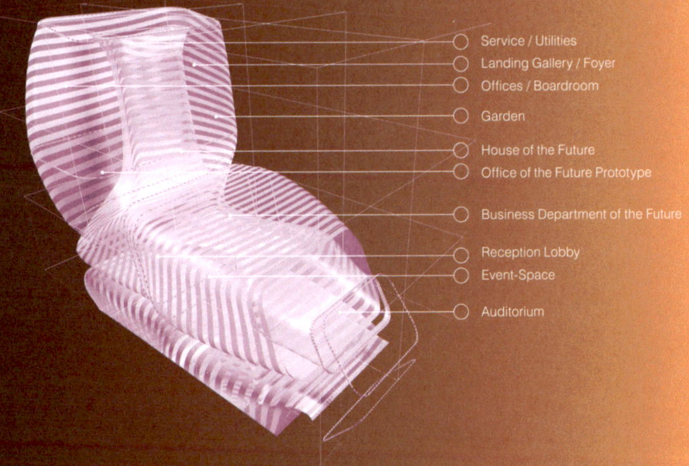
Service / Utilities
Landing Gallery / Foyer
Offices / Boardroom
Garden
House of the Future
Office of the Future Prototype
Business Department of the Future
Reception Lobby
Event-Space
Auditorium

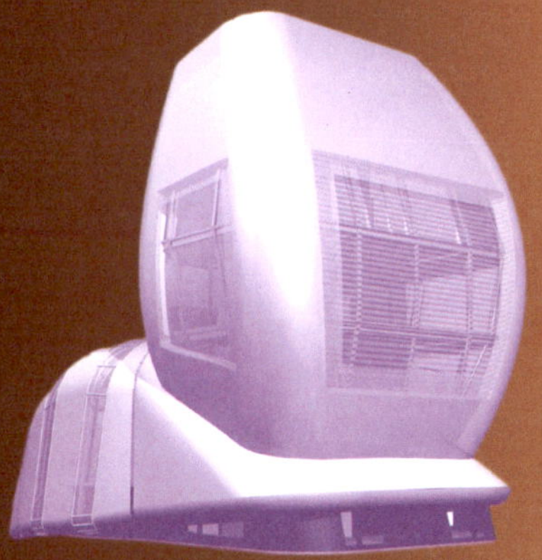

MÖBIUS HOUSE

Het Gooi (NL)

06

00
12
18
sleeping
living 02
working 01
working 01
living 02
sleeping
working 02
living 01

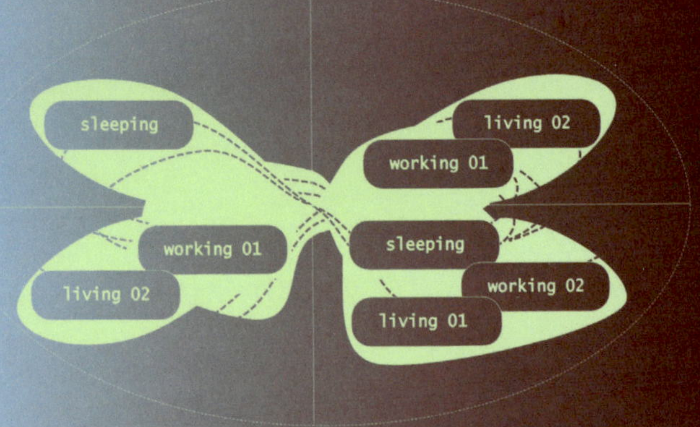

sleeping

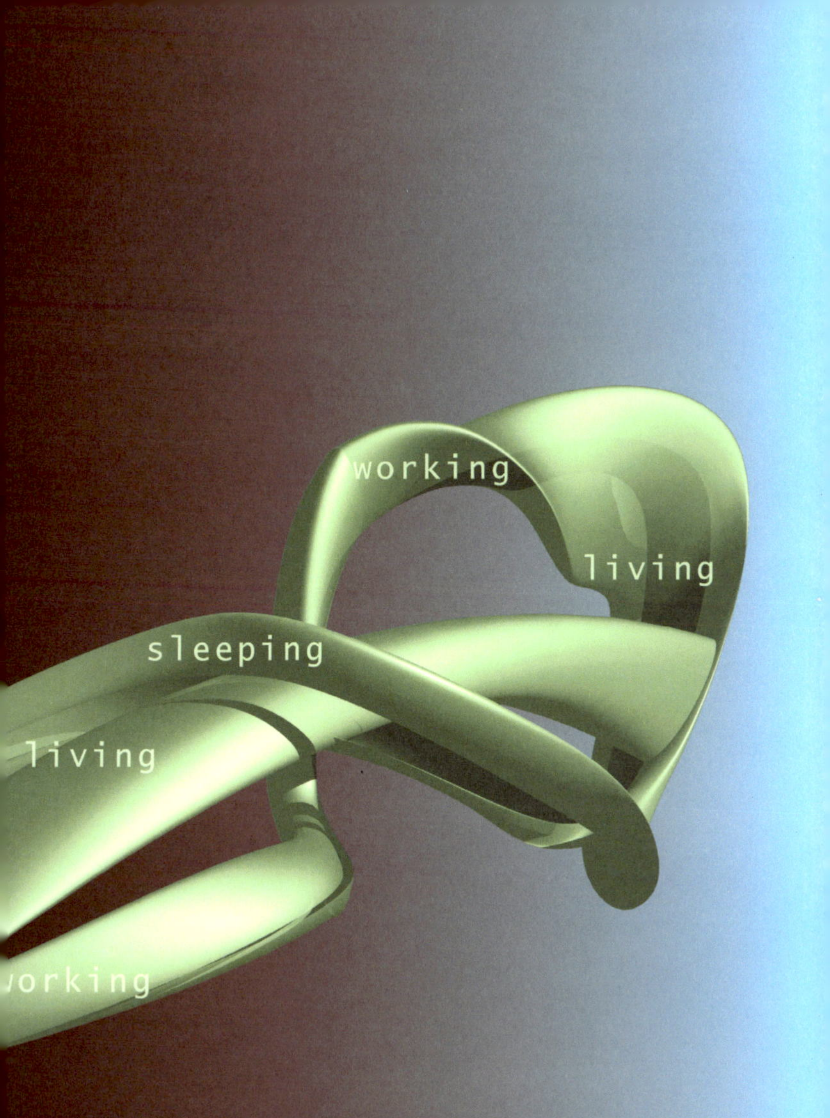

working

living

sleeping

living

orking

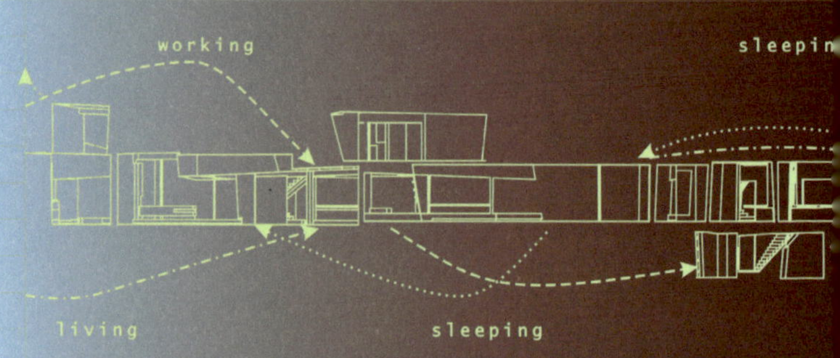
working
sleepin
living
sleeping

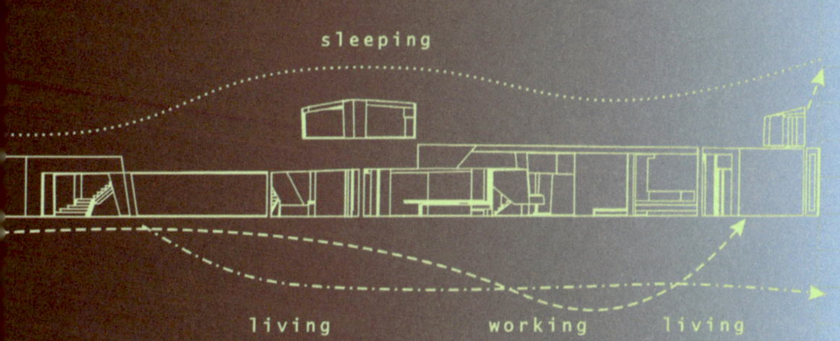
sleeping
living
working
living

THE ELLIPSICOON

Manila (PH)

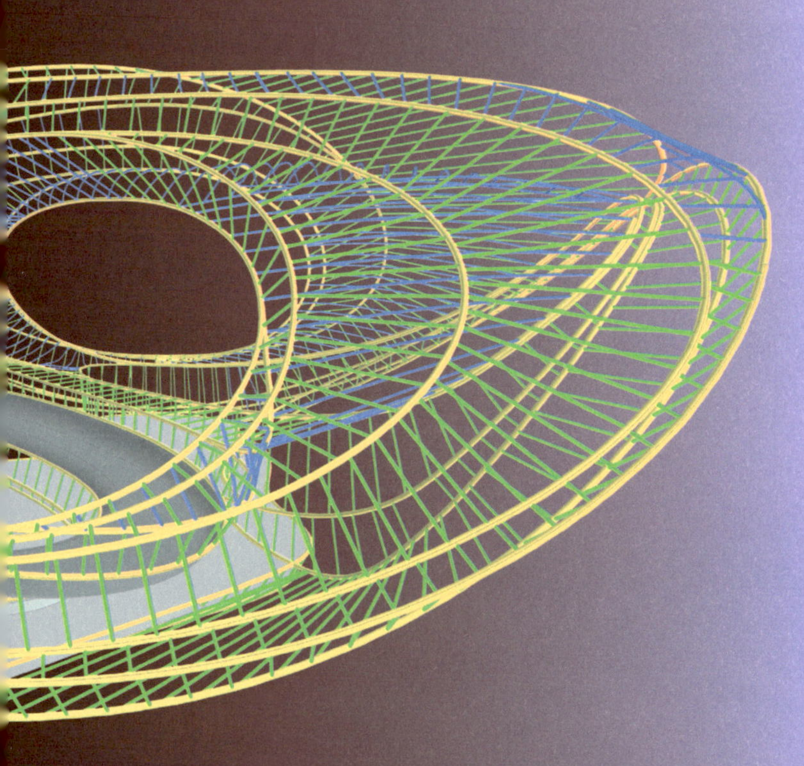

THE CHANGING ROOM

Venice Biennale (IT)

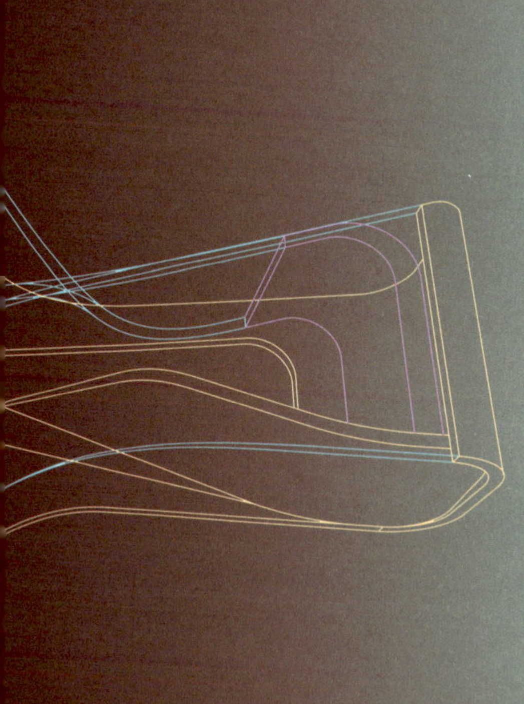

CENTRE FOR VIRTUAL ENGINEERING (ZVE)

Stuttgart (DE)

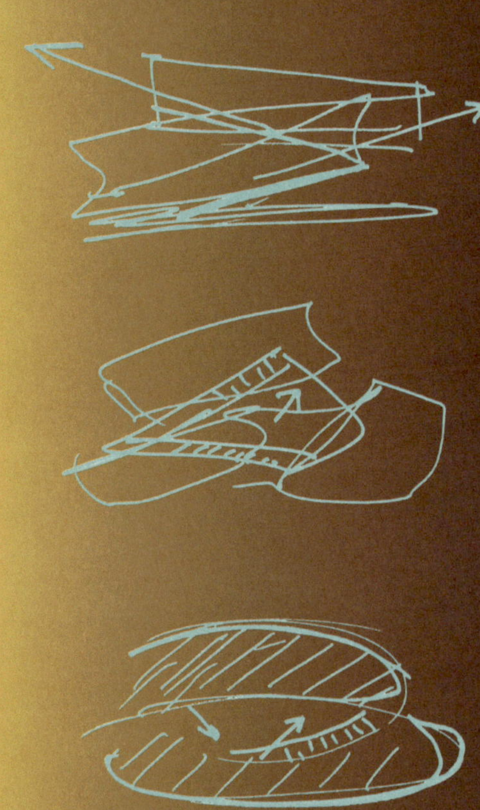

spatial configuration

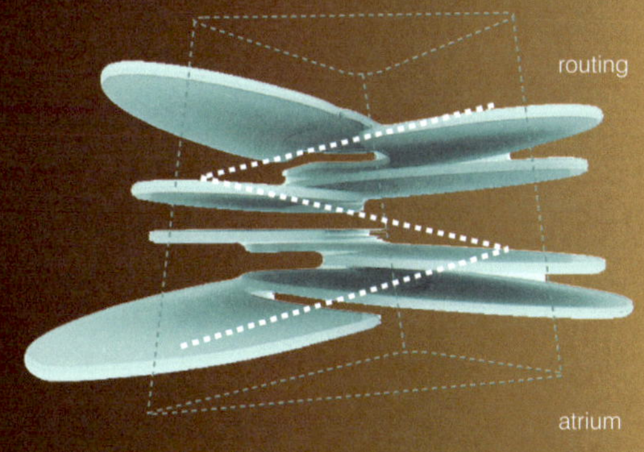

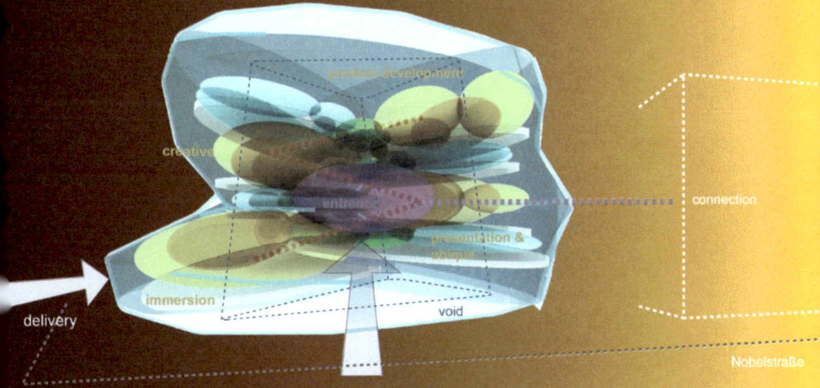

EDUCATION EXECUTIVE AGENCY & TAX OFFICES

Groningen (NL)

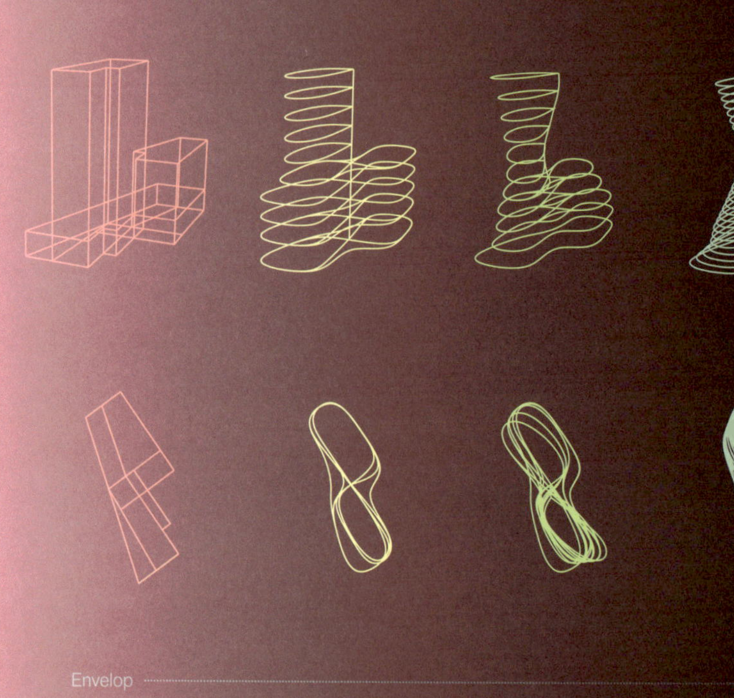

Envelop

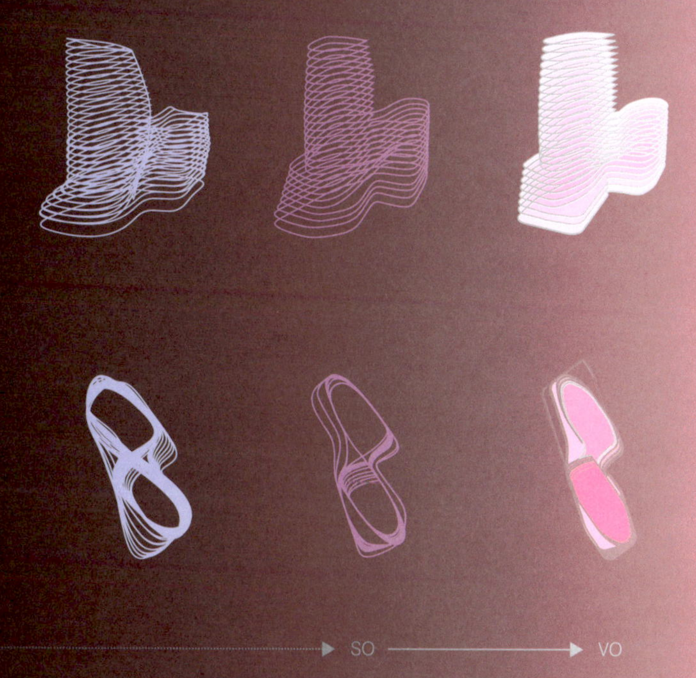
SO
VO

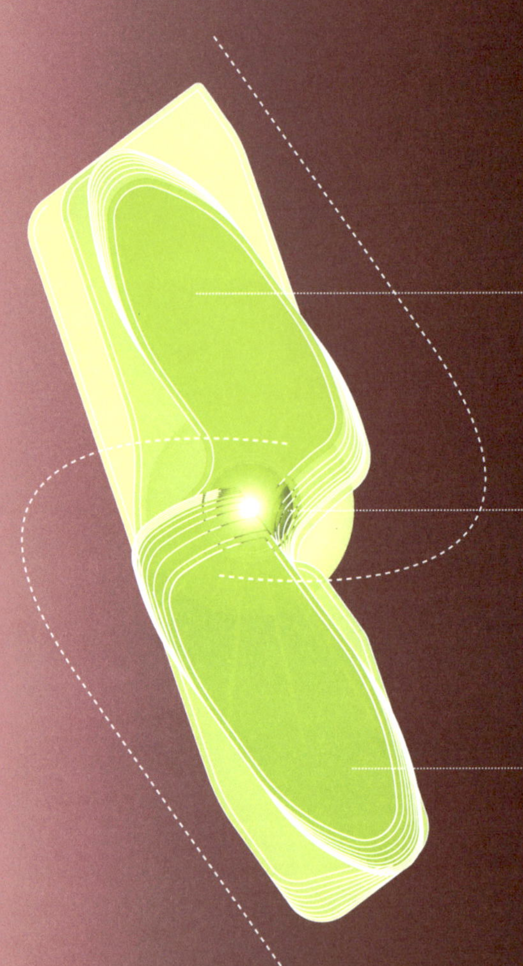
user A
merging
identities
user B

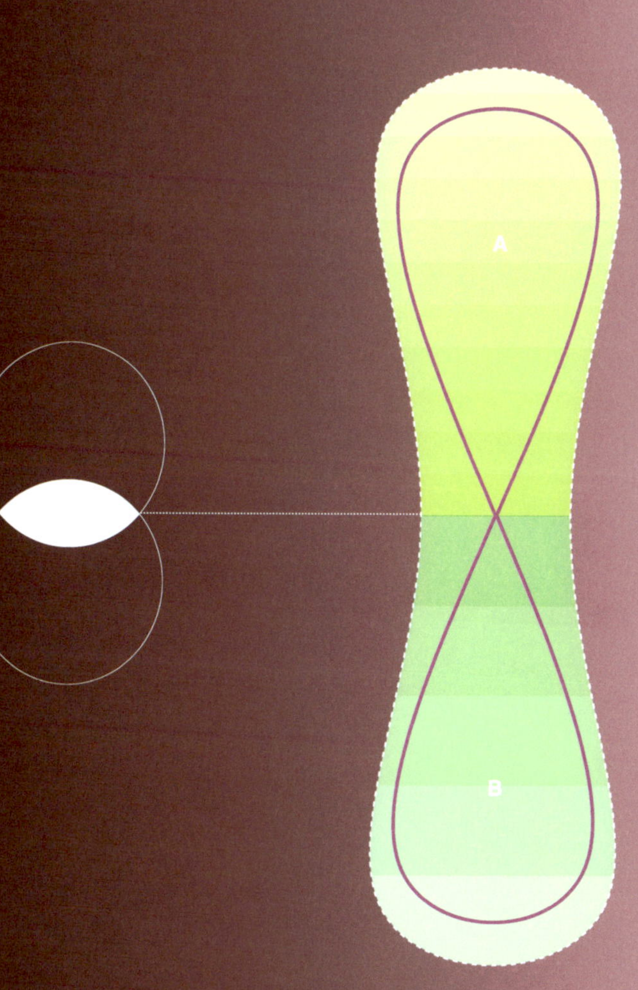
A
B

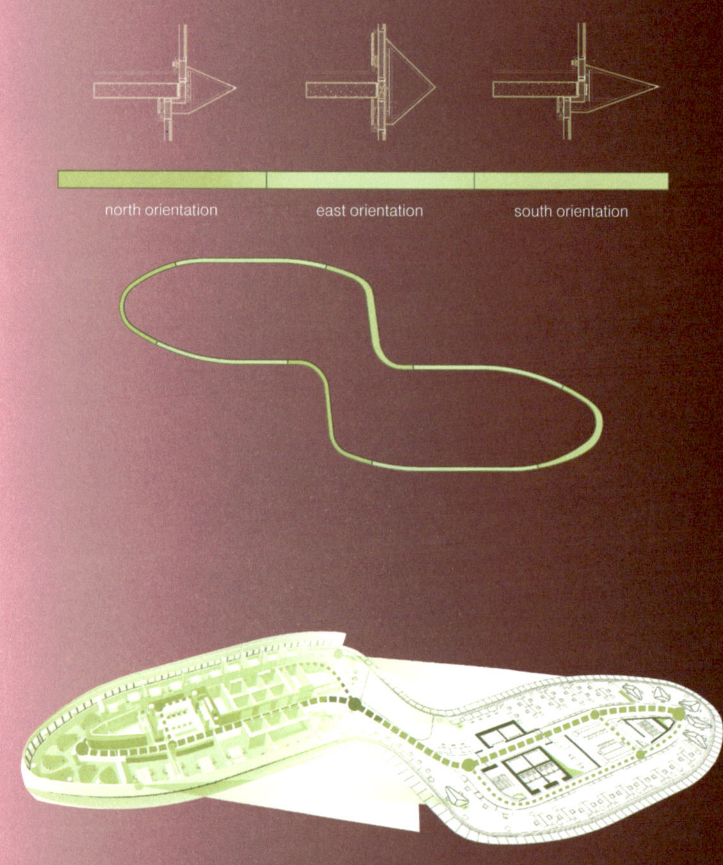
north orientation
east orientation
south orientation

2 THE STRUCTURE OF MOVEMENT

nmr FACILITY

Utrecht (NL)

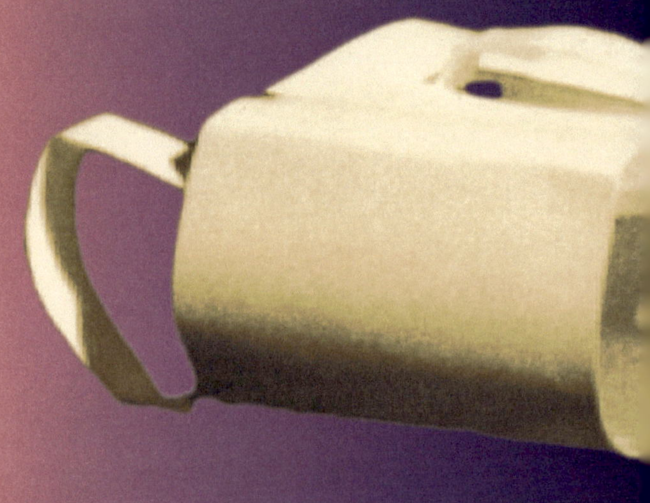

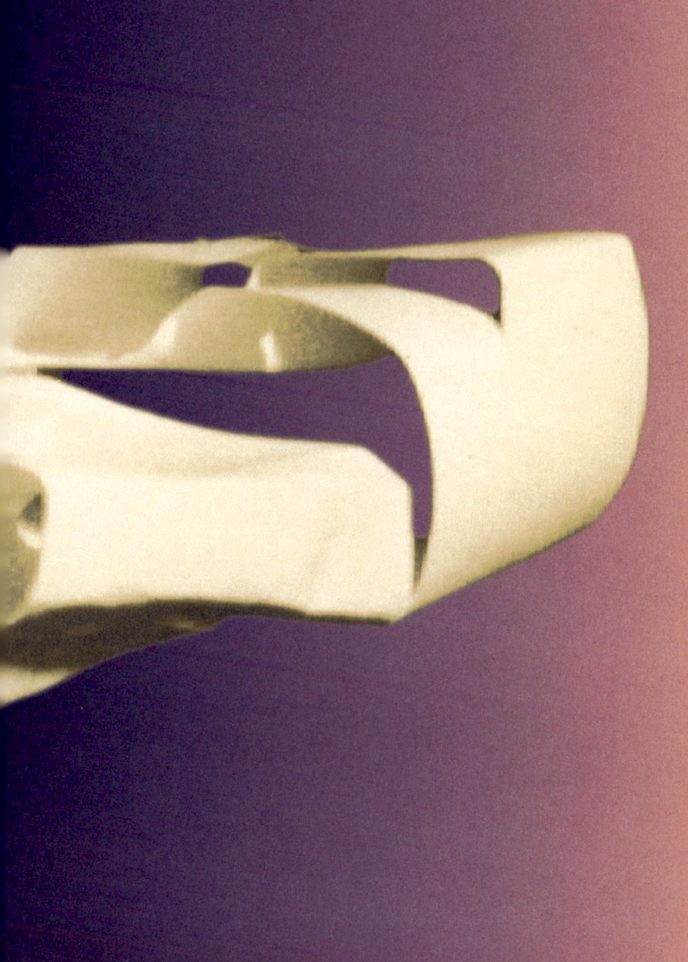

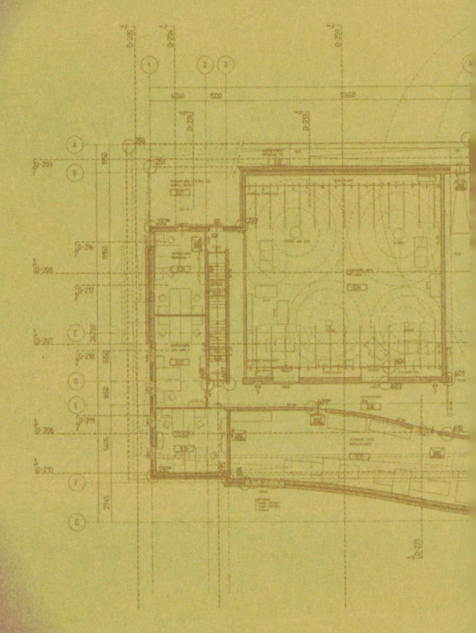

THE VALKHOF MUSEUM

Nijmegen (NL)

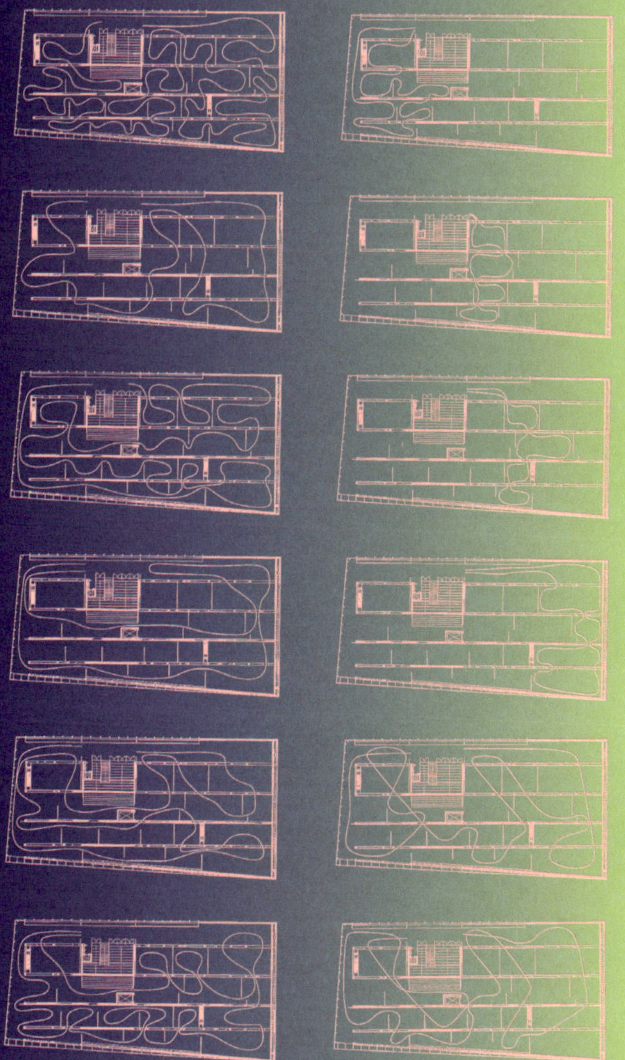

NATIONAL ART MUSEUM OF CHINA (NAMOC)

Beijing (CN)

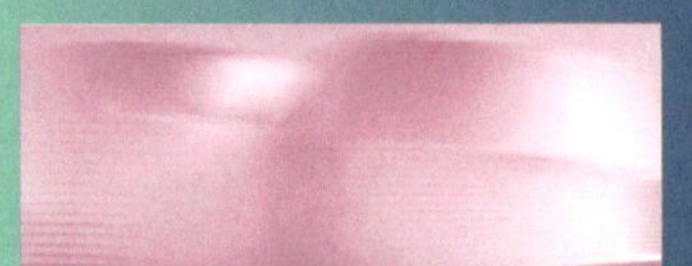

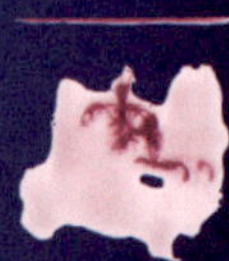

day

still

white paper

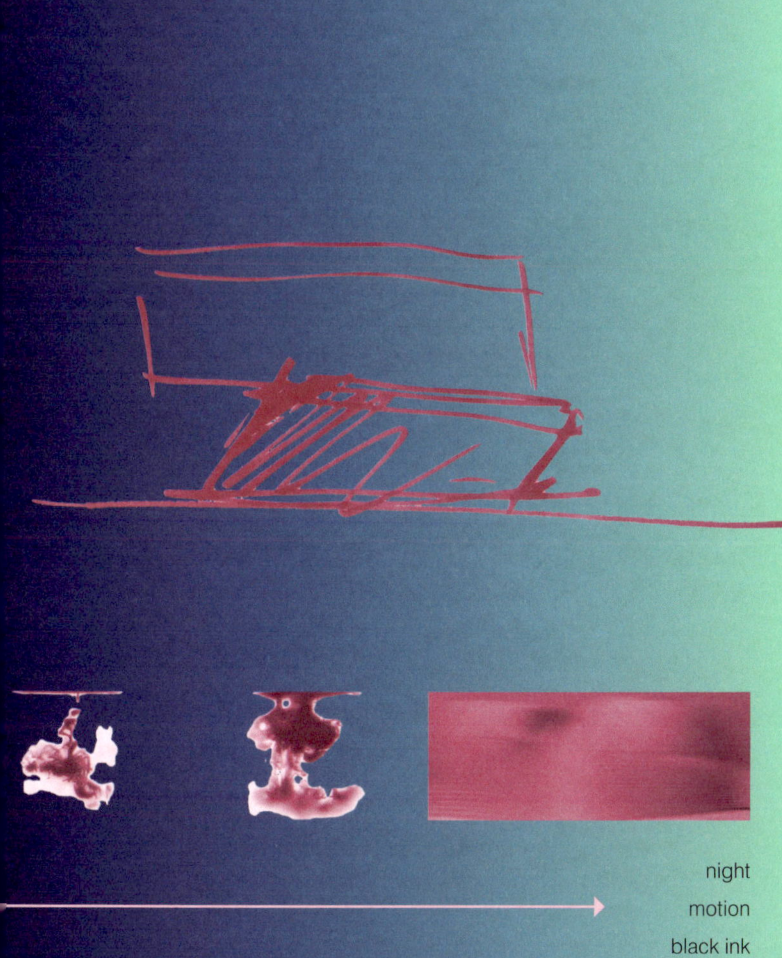

night

motion

black ink

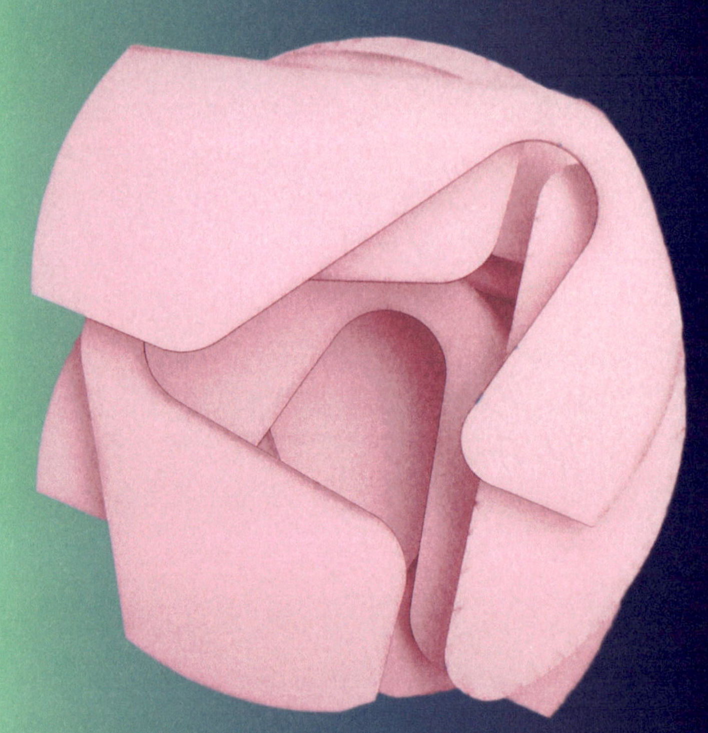

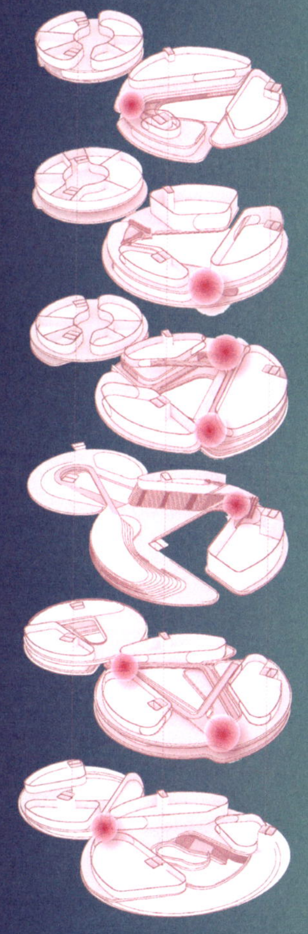

NODE POSITIONS ISOMETRY

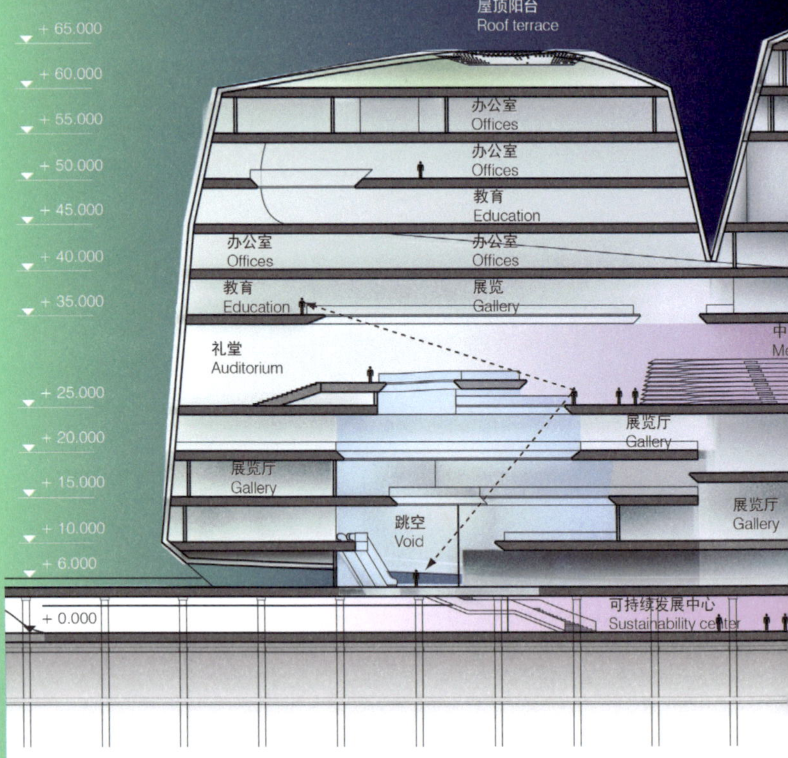

LONGITUDINAL SECTION

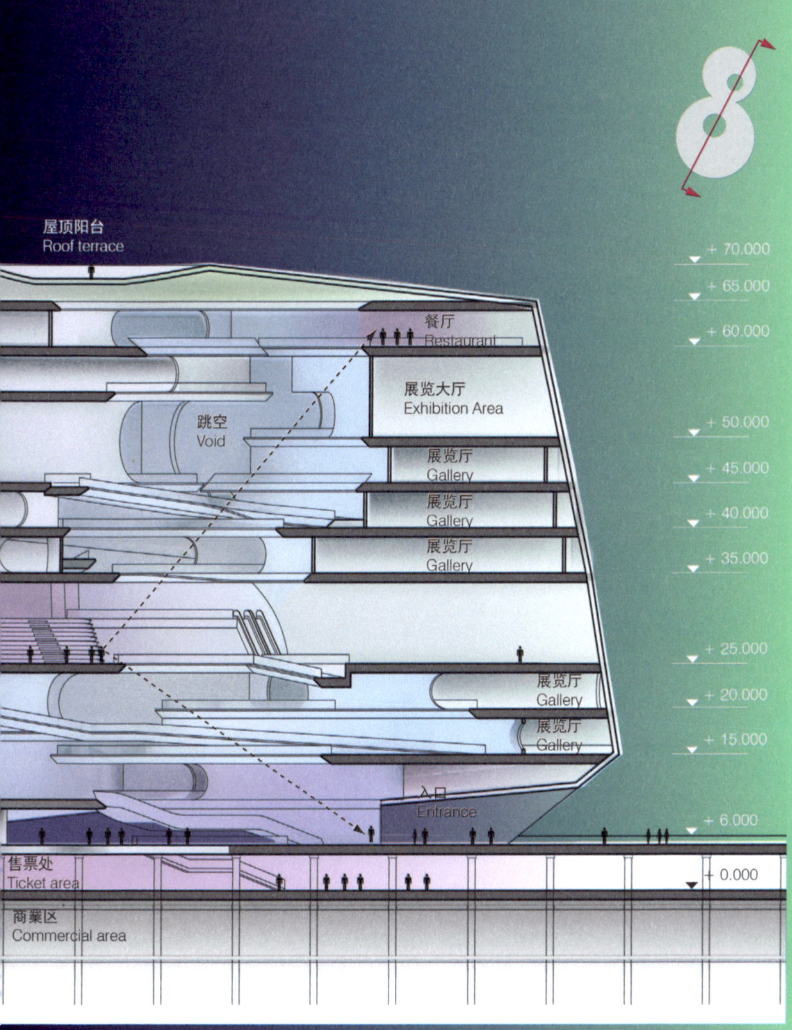
8
屋顶阳台
Roof terrace
+ 70.000
+ 65.000
+ 60.000
餐厅
Restaurant
展览大厅
Exhibition Area
跳空
Void
+ 50.000
展览厅
Gallery
+ 45.000
展览厅
Gallery
+ 40.000
展览厅
Gallery
+ 35.000
+ 25.000
展览厅
Gallery
+ 20.000
展览厅
Gallery
+ 15.000
入口
Entrance
+ 6.000
售票处
Ticket area
+ 0.000
商業区
Commercial area

OPPO FLAGSHIP STORE

Guangzhou (CN)

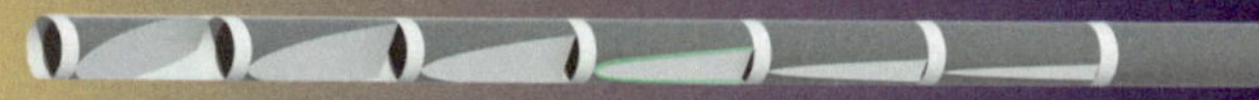

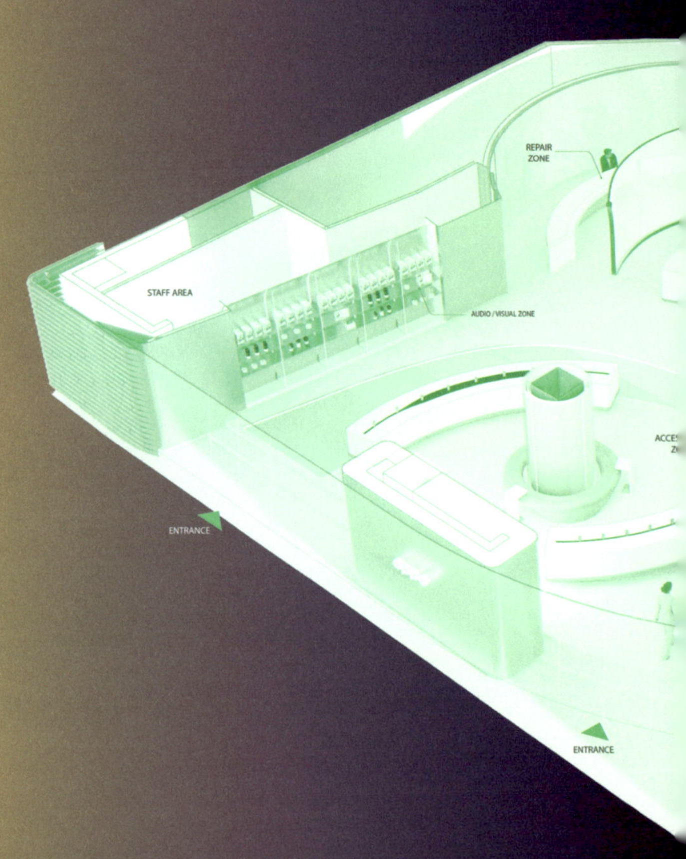
REPAIR
ZONE
STAFF AREA
AUDIO / VISUAL ZONE
ENTRANCE
ENTRANCE

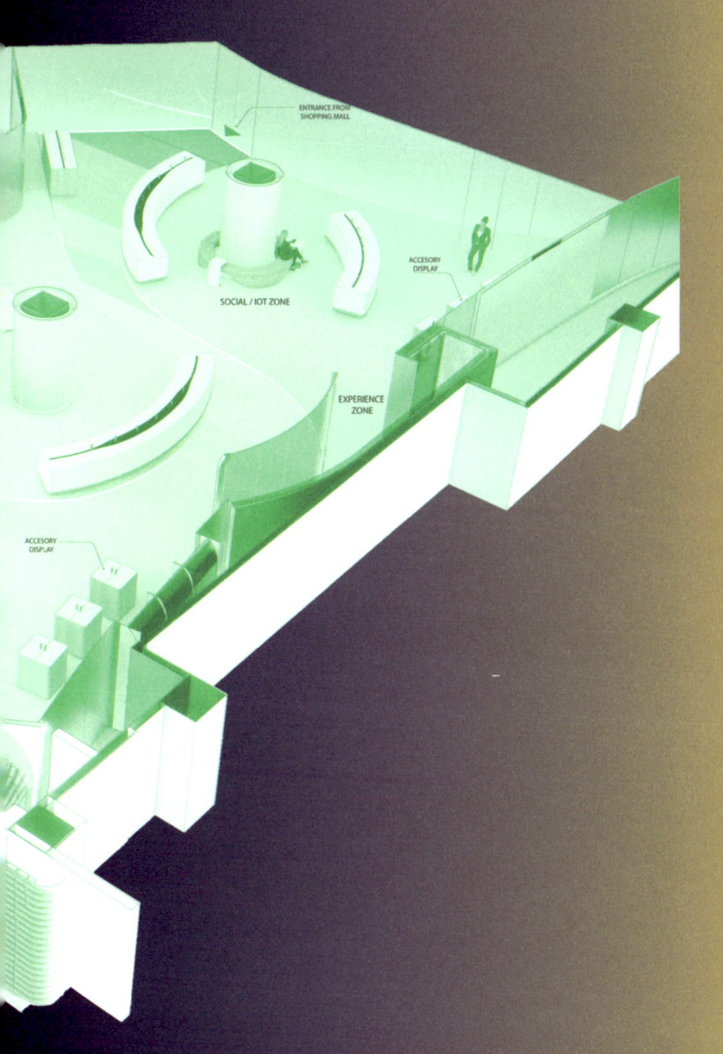
ENTRANCE FROM
SHOPPING MALL
ACCESORY
DISPLAY
SOCIAL / IOT ZONE
EXPERIENCE
ZONE
ACCESORY
DISPLAY

OPPO
X
oppo

oppo
oppo

UNX2
United Nude

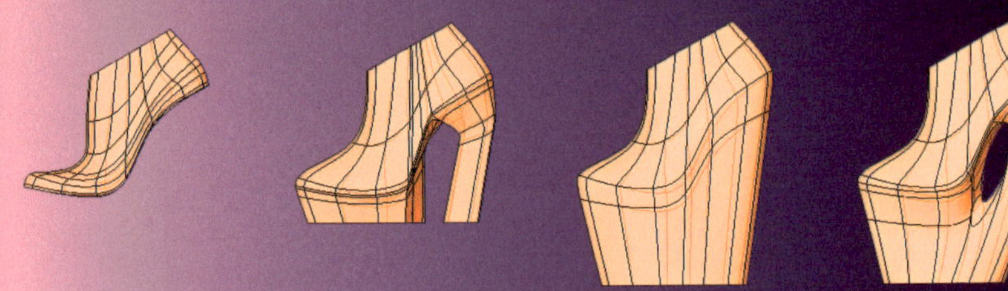

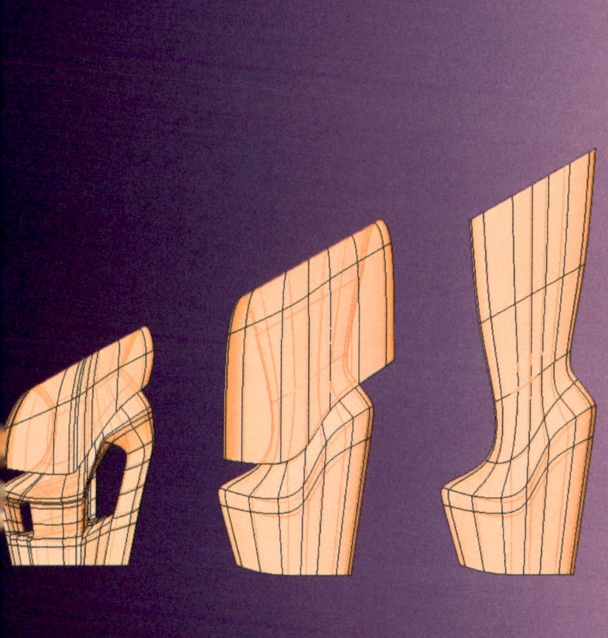

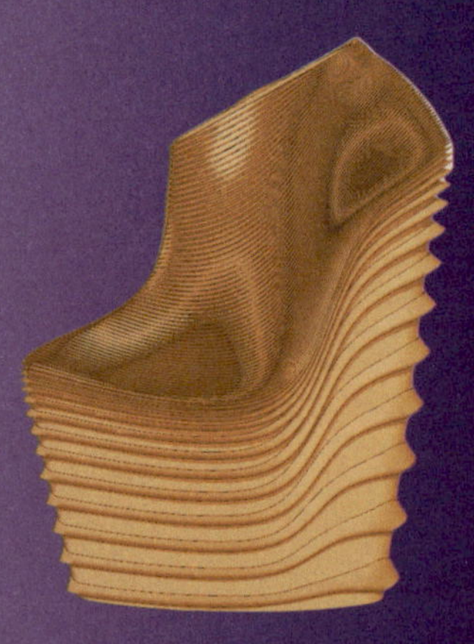

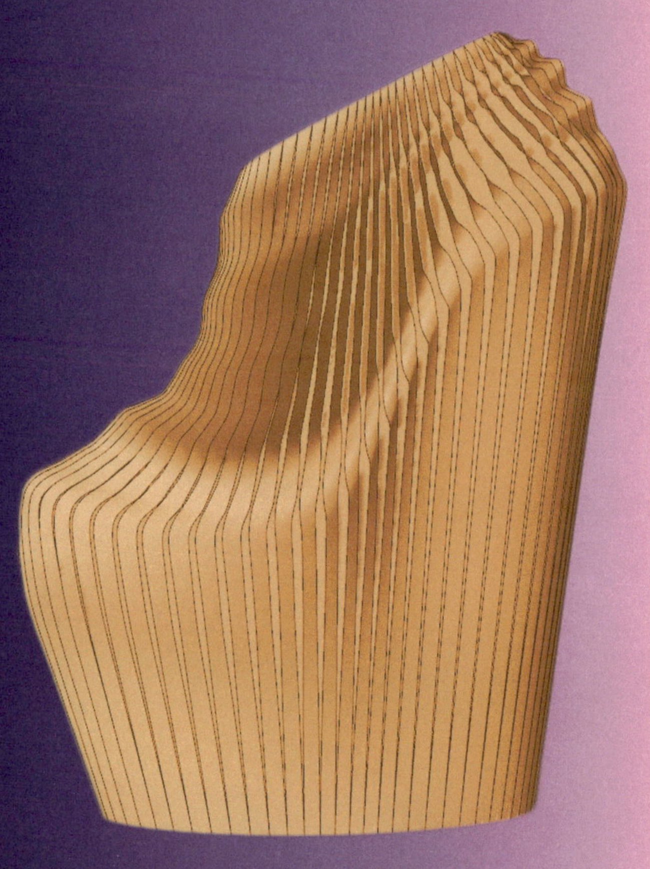

3 BLOB TO BOX

MUMUTH MUSIC THEATRE

Graz (AT)

THEATRE AGORA

Lelystad (NL)

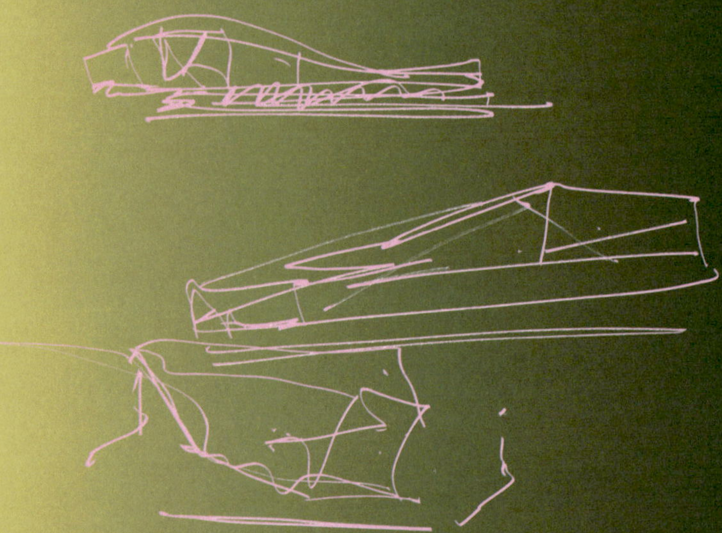

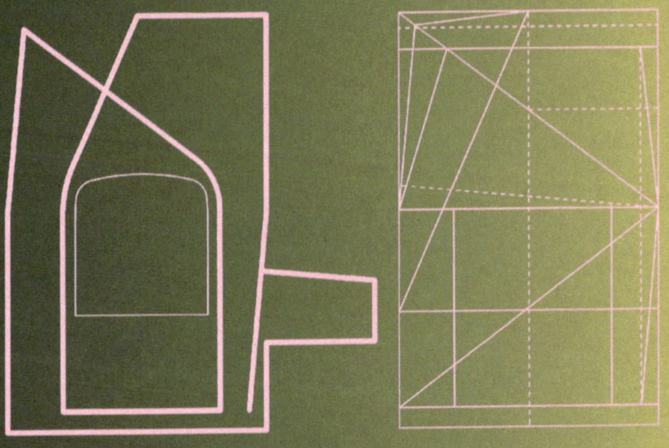

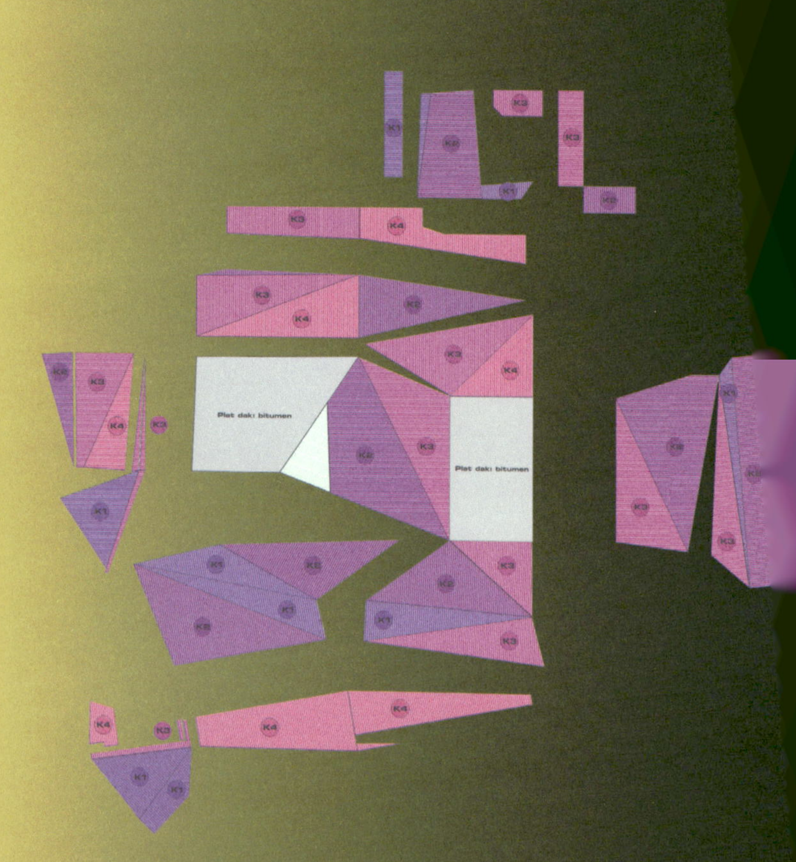
Plat dak: bitumen
Plat dak: bitumen

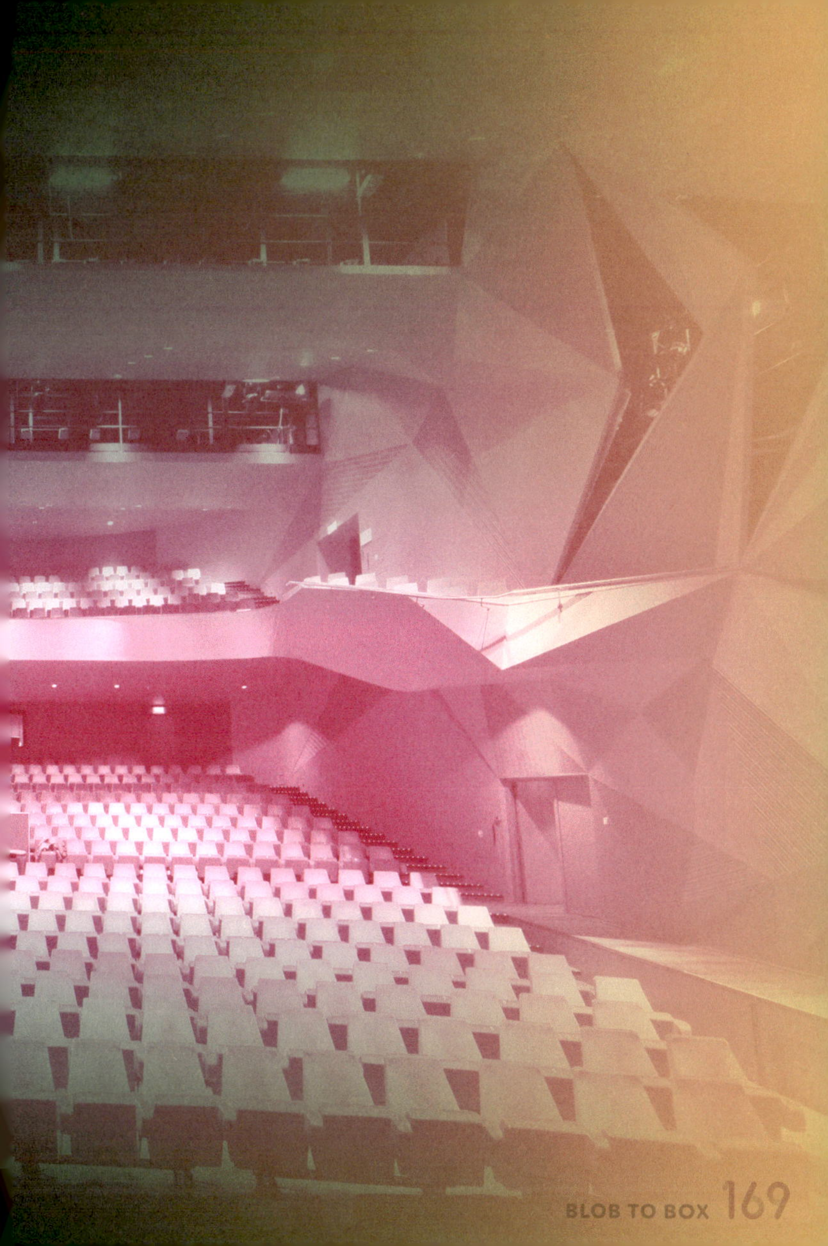

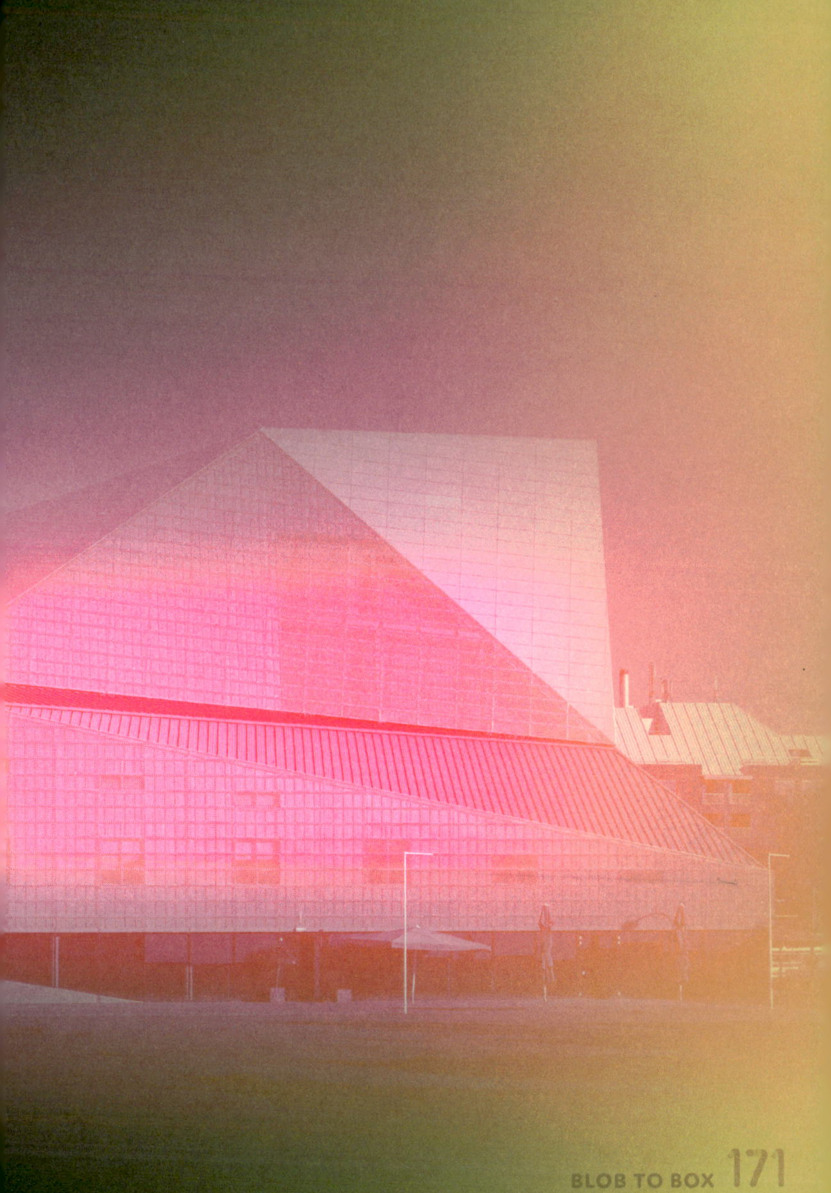

ECHO

TU Delft (NL)

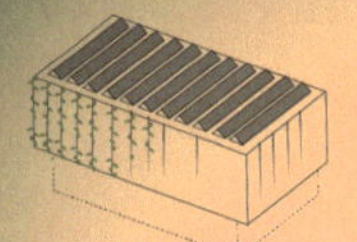

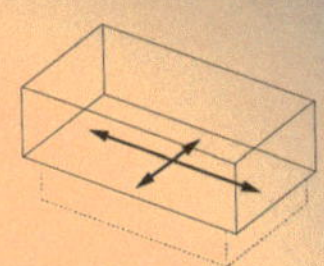

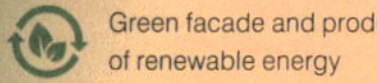

Flexibility, future-proof by large spans

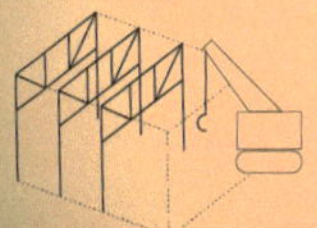

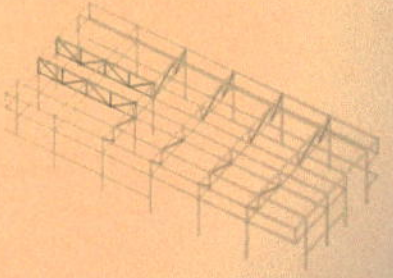

Demountable building system with steel structure

Parametric structural model for digital optimisation

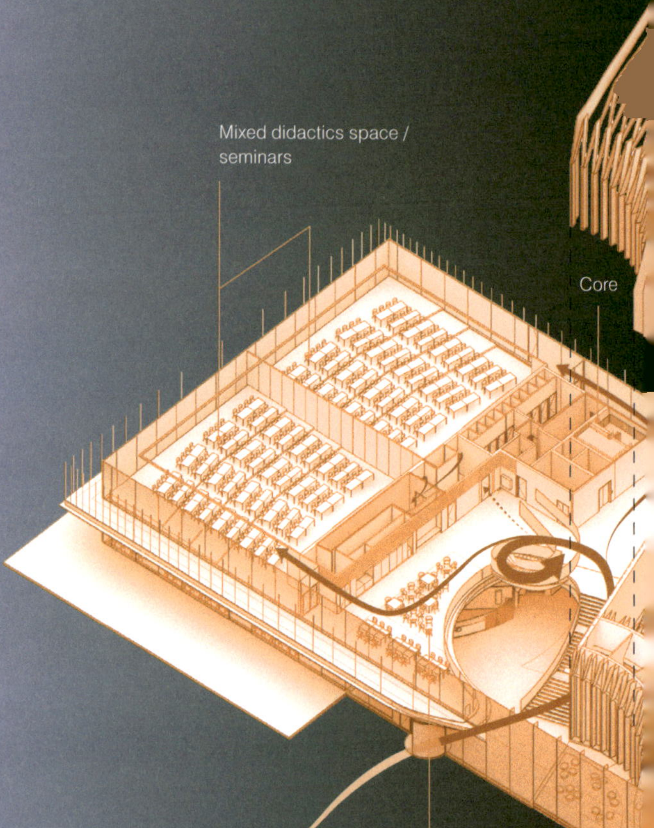

Mixed didactics space / seminars

Core

Study workspace type B

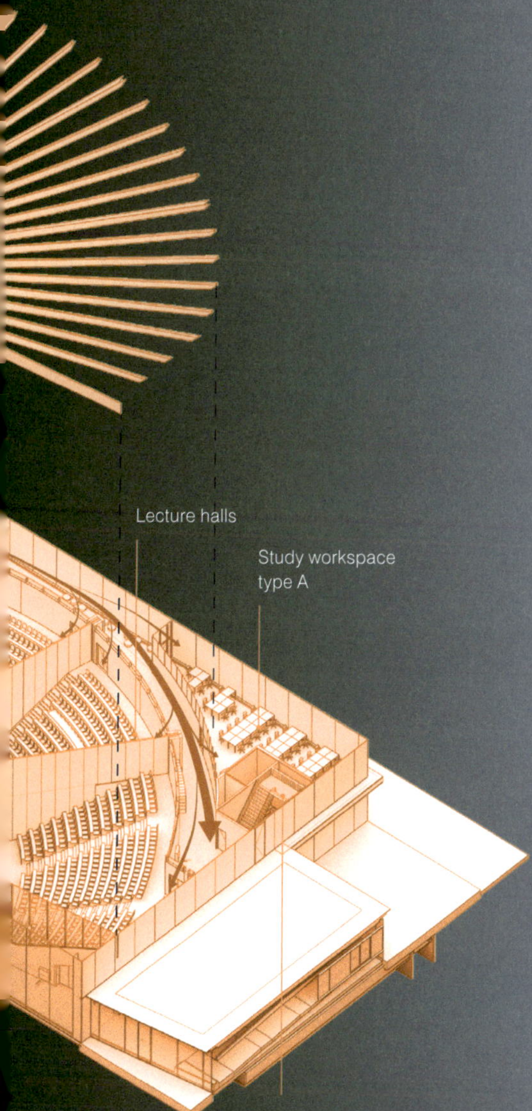

Lecture halls

Study workspace type A

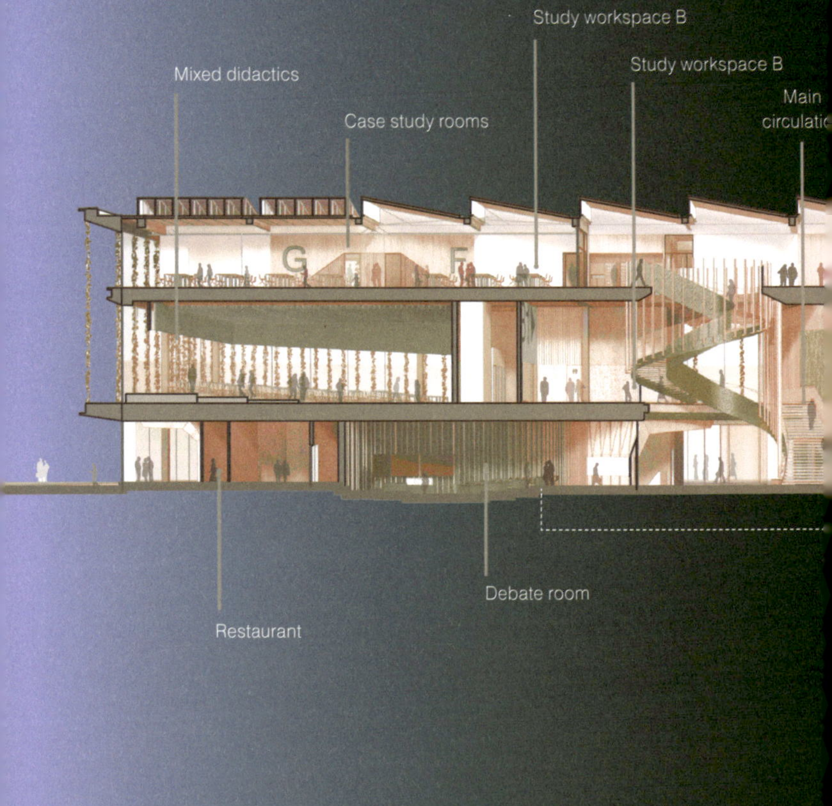

Study workspace B

Mixed didactics

Study workspace B

Main circulatic

Case study rooms

Debate room

Restaurant

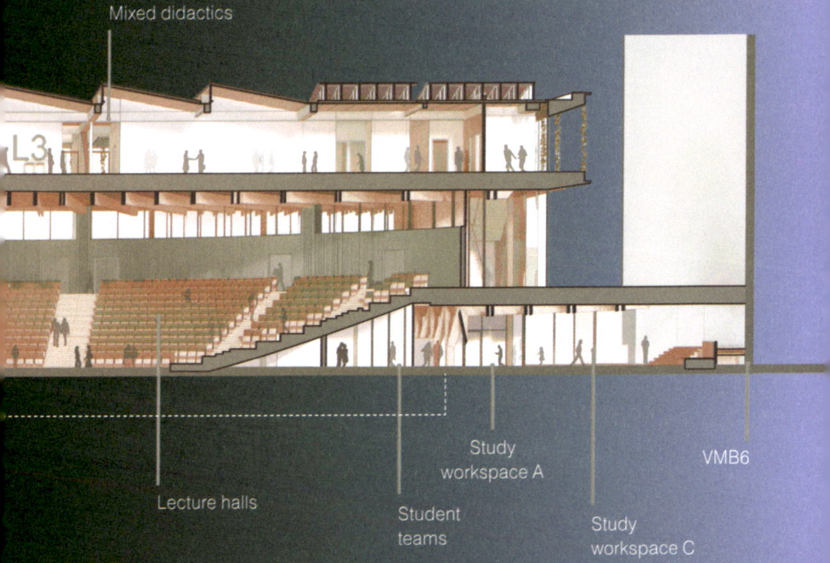

Mixed didactics

L3

Lecture halls

Student teams

Study workspace A

Study workspace C

VMB6

TU

LOUIS VUITTON FLAGSHIP STORE

Osaka (JP)

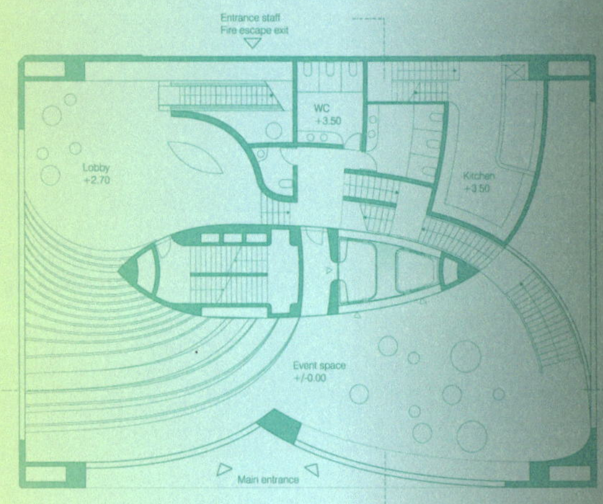
Entrance staff
Fire escape exit
WC
+3.50
Lobby
+2.70
Kitchen
+3.50
Car entrance
Event space
+/-0.00
Main entrance

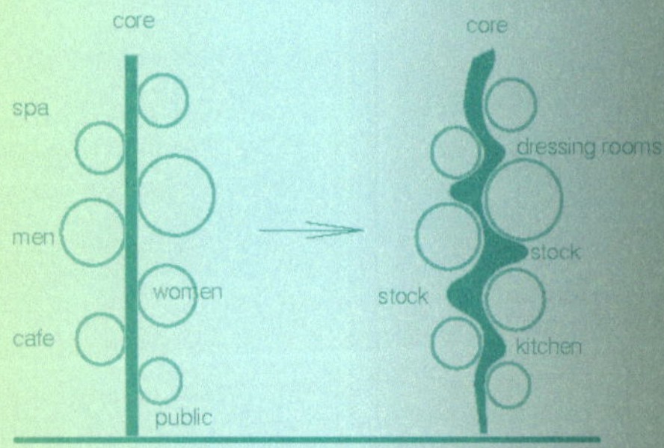
core
spa
men
women
cafe
public
core
dressing rooms
stock
stock
kitchen
extension of the core

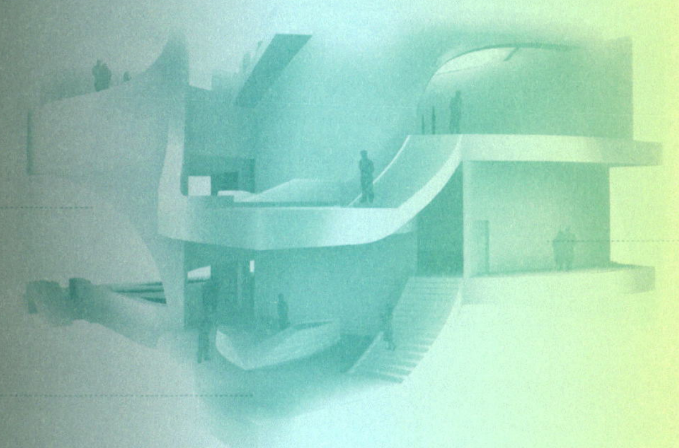

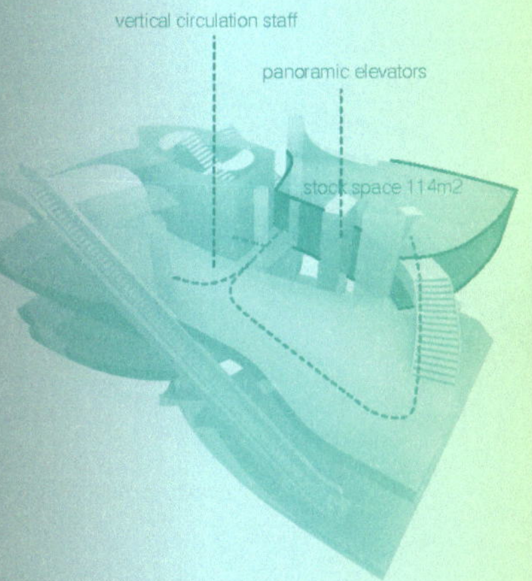
vertical circulation staff
panoramic elevators
stock space 114m2

escalator
diagonal movement
upwards
stairs
diagonal movement
up and downwards
elevator
vertical movement
up and downwards

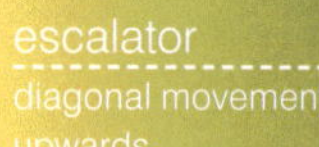

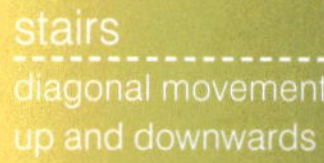

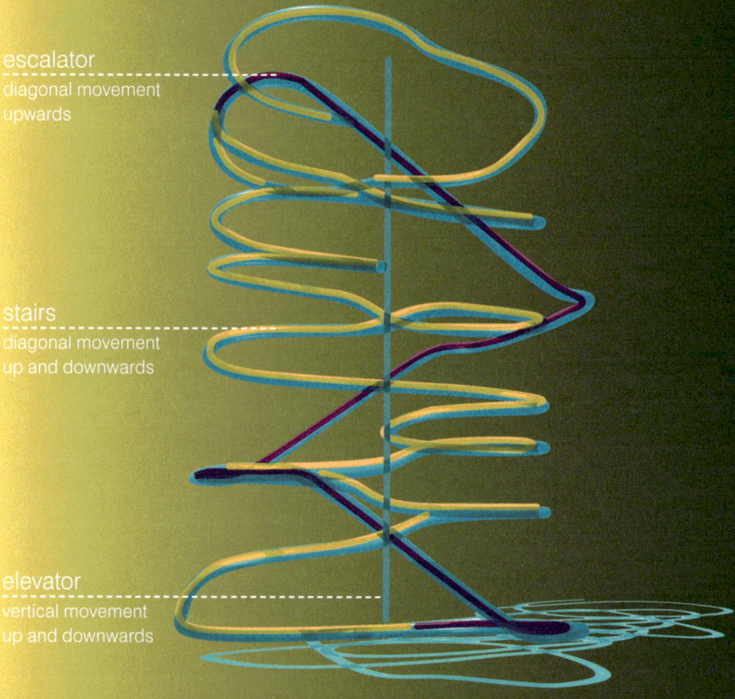

4

V-MODEL

ARNHEM CENTRAL STATION CAR PARK

Arnhem (NL)

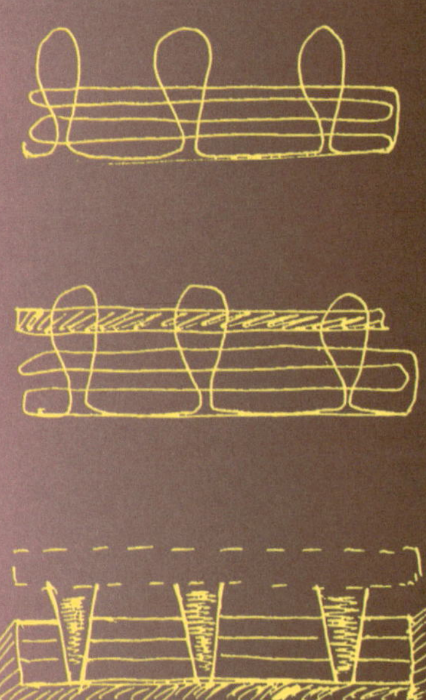

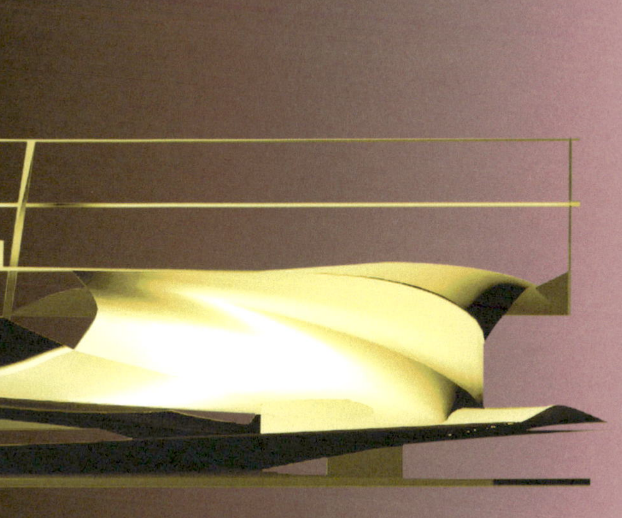

25
25

WIEN MITTE URBAN COMPETITION

Vienna (AT)

Einleitung der Vertikallasten

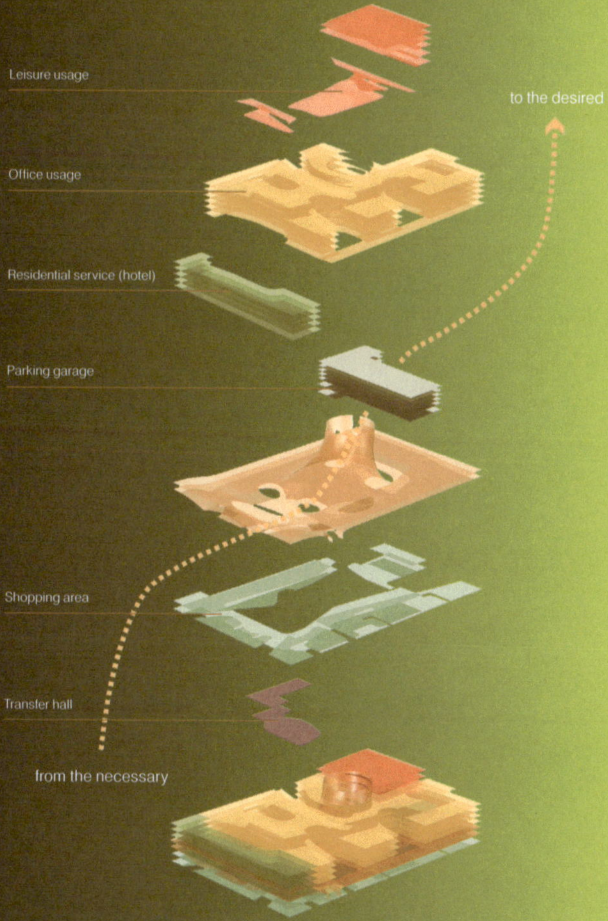

Leisure usage

to the desired

Office usage

Residential service (hotel)

Parking garage

Shopping area

Transfer hall

from the necessary

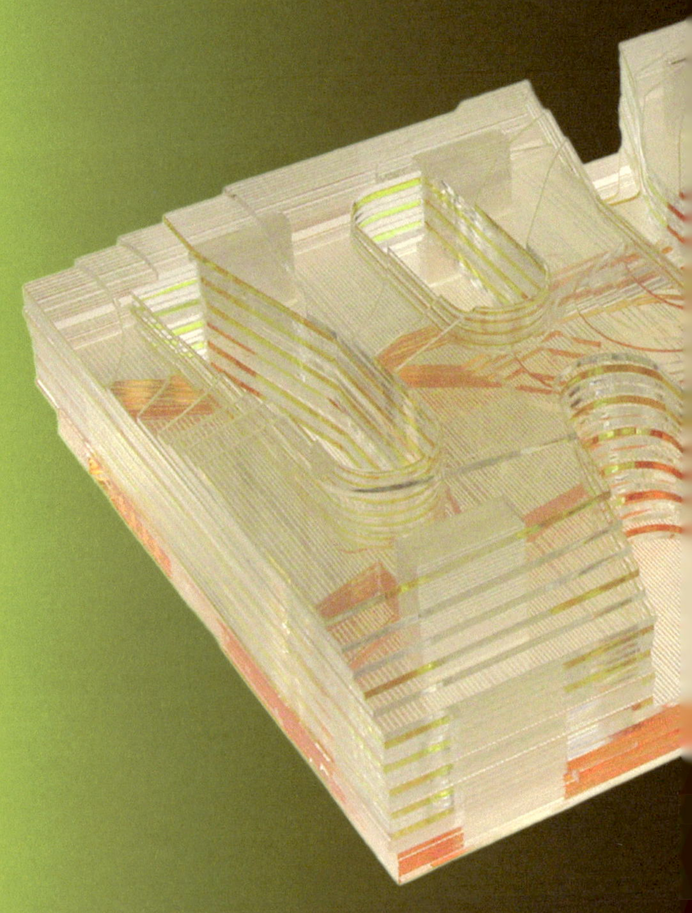

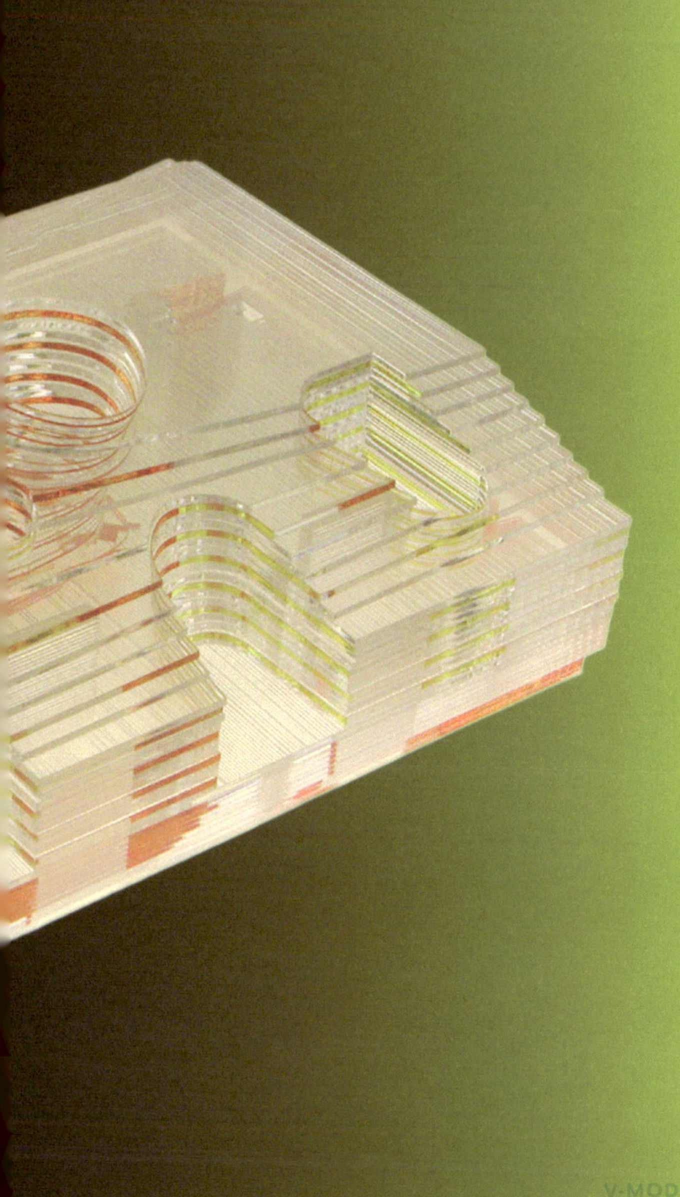

5 CROSSING POINTS

BURNHAM PAVILION

Chicago (US)

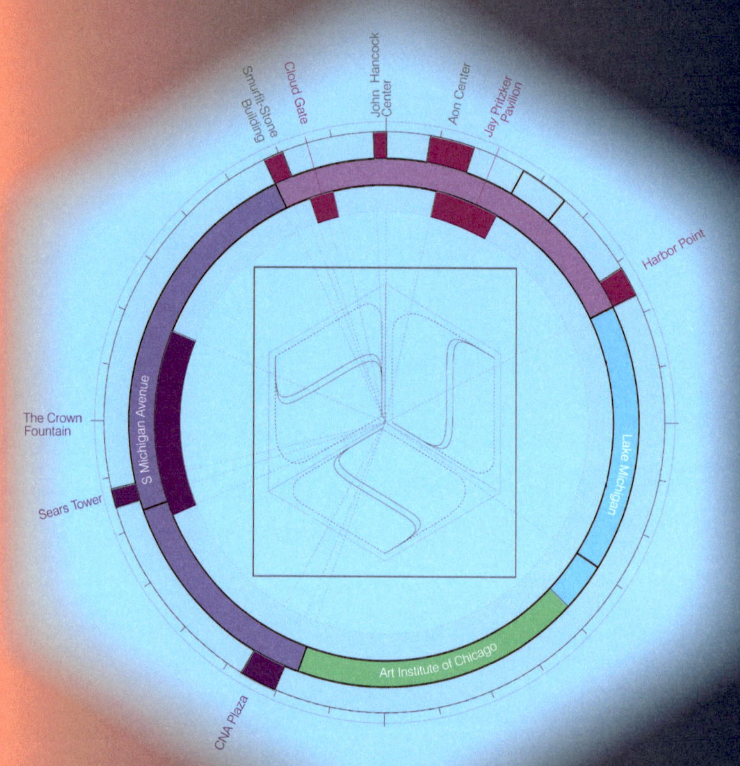

Views and orientation

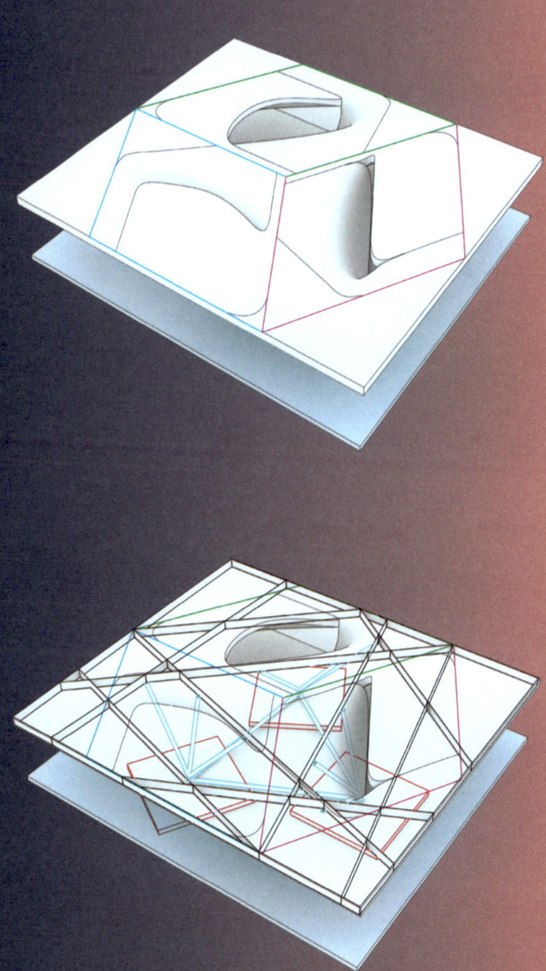

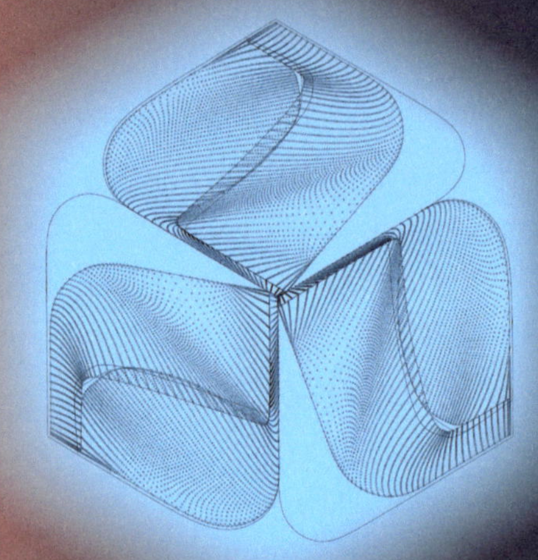

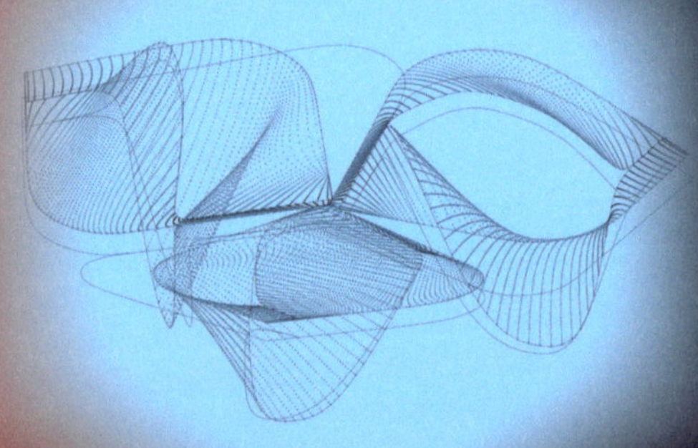

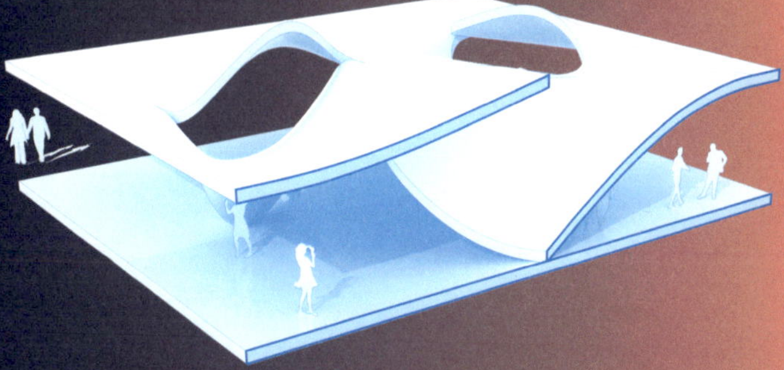

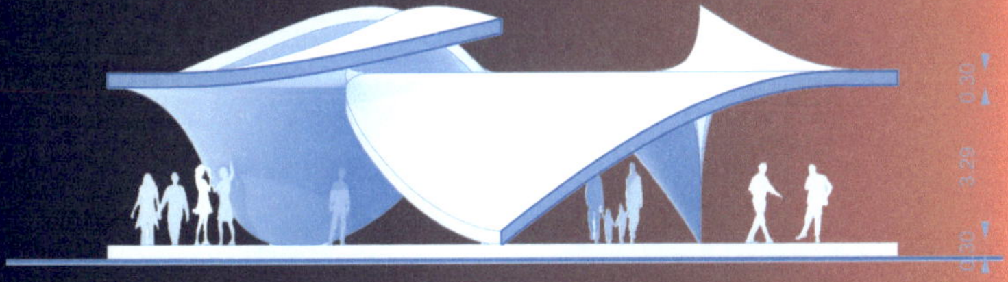

0.30
3.29
0.30

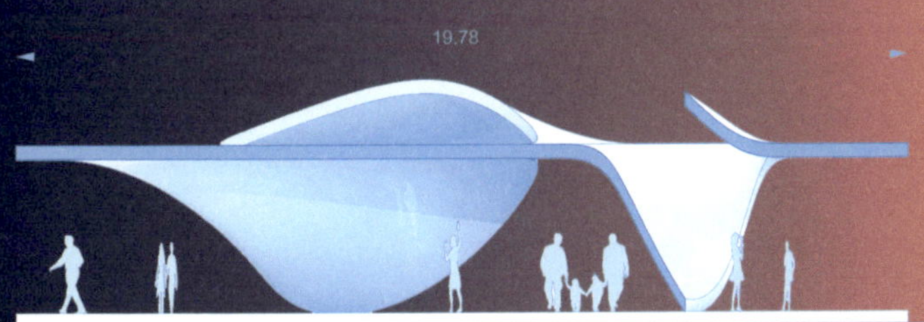

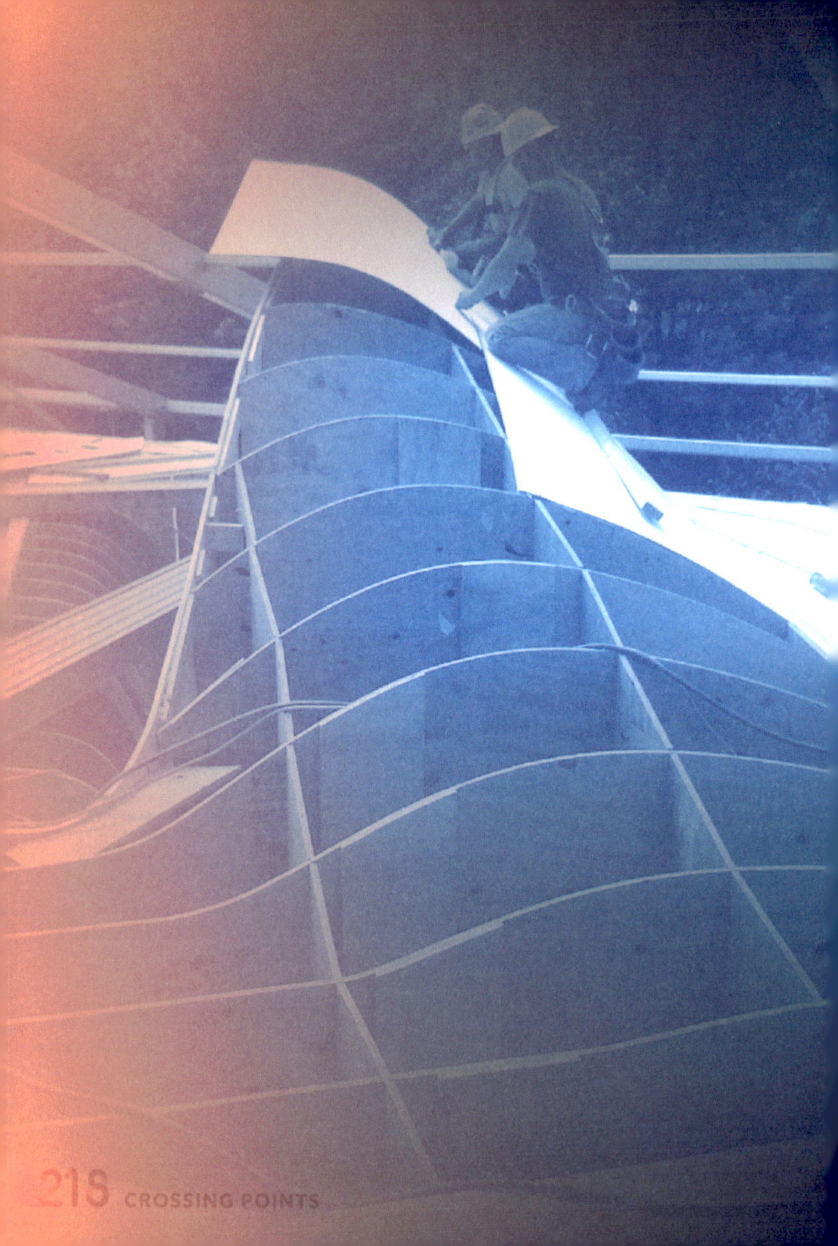

THE W.I.N.D. HOUSE

North Holland (NL)

Landscape becoming building

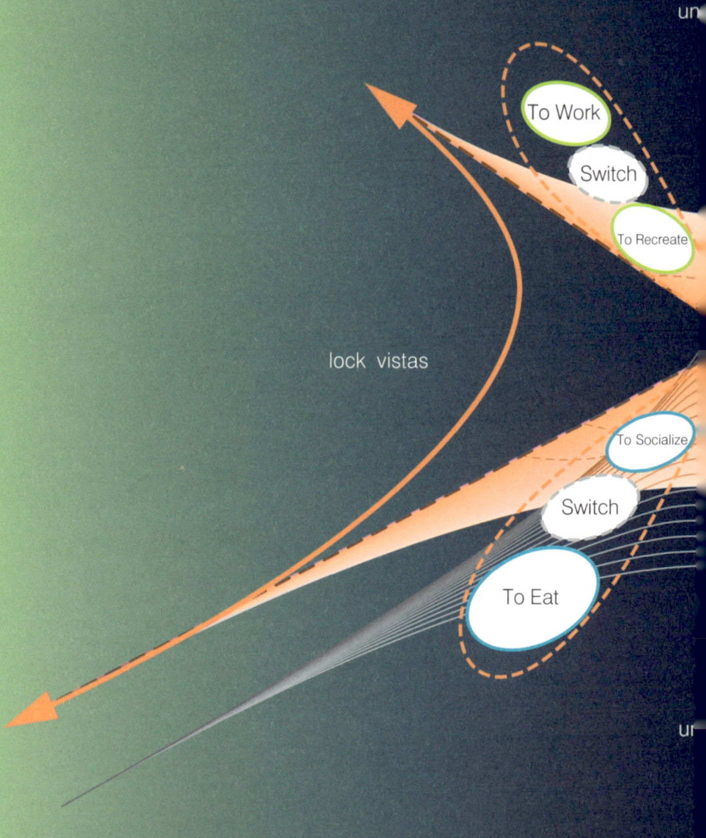

un

To Work

Switch

To Recreate

lock vistas

To Socialize

Switch

To Eat

u

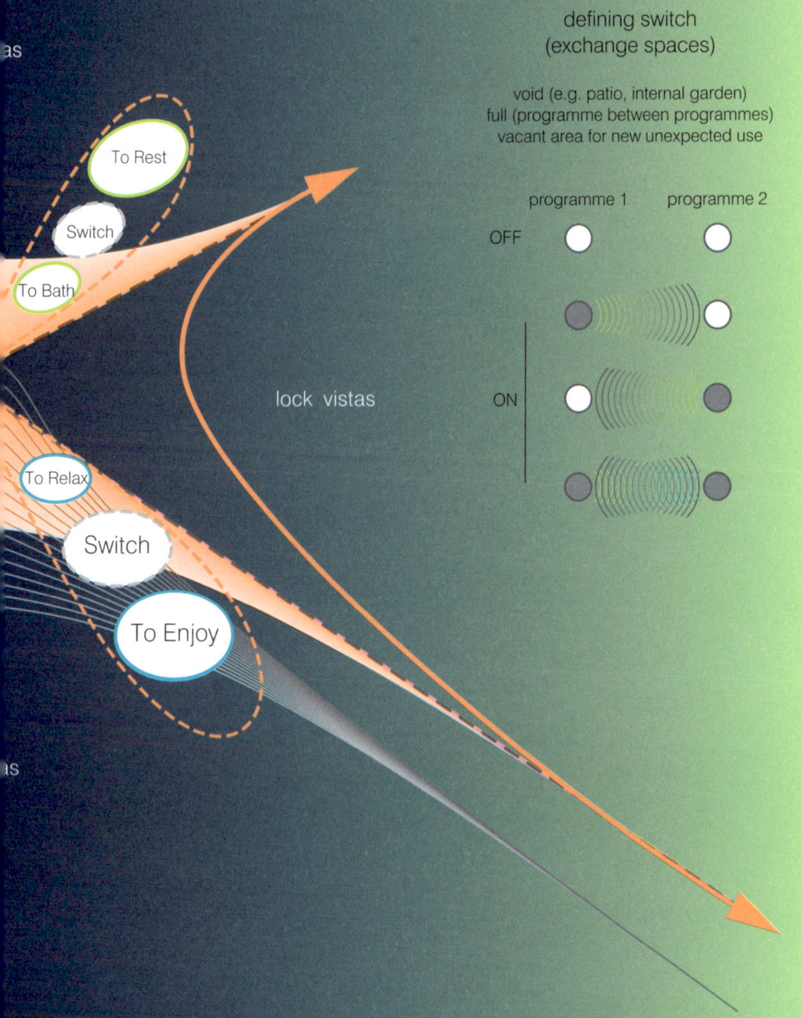

as

To Rest

Switch

To Bath

lock vistas

To Relax

Switch

To Enjoy

as

defining switch
(exchange spaces)

void (e.g. patio, internal garden)
full (programme between programmes)
vacant area for new unexpected use

programme 1 programme 2

OFF

ON

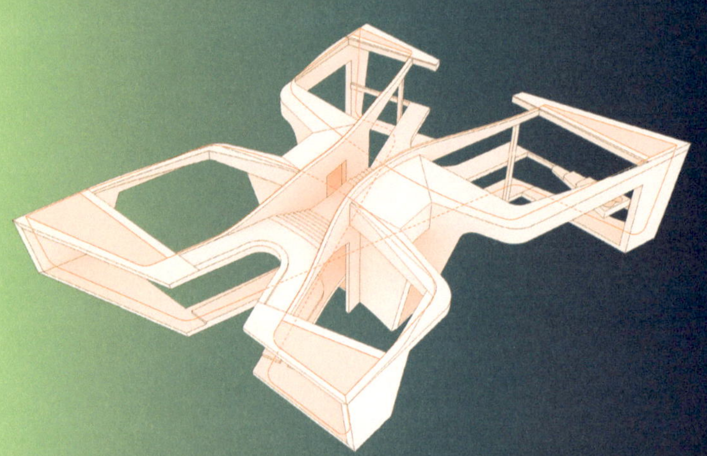

2
3
4
6
7
8
9
9
10
10

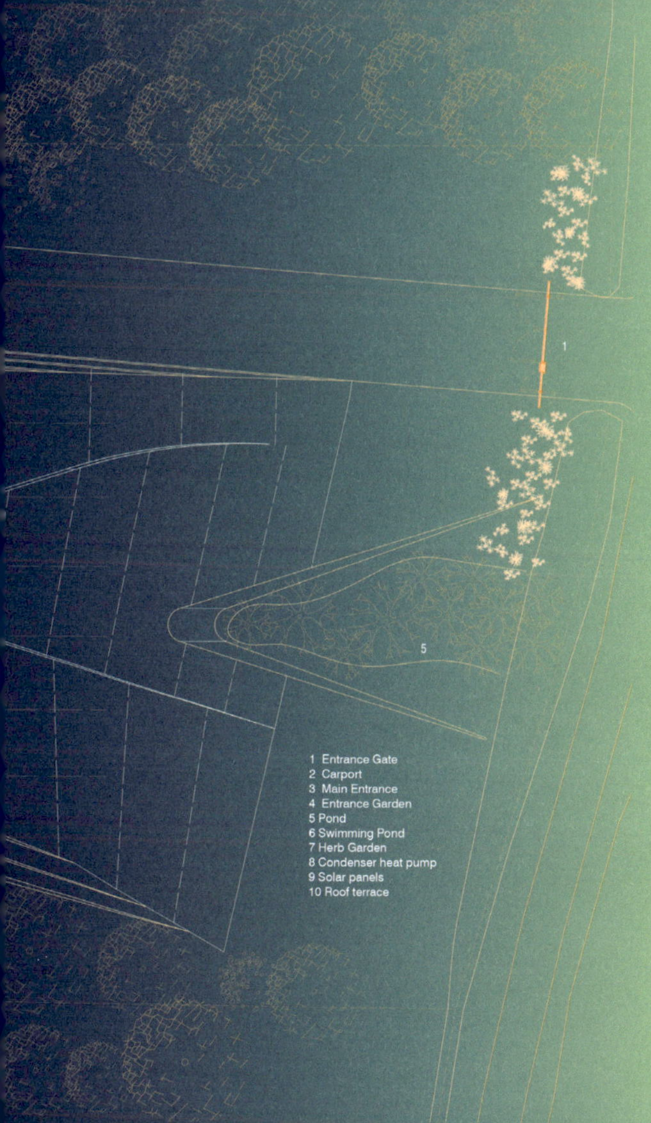
1
5
1 Entrance Gate
2 Carport
3 Main Entrance
4 Entrance Garden
5 Pond
6 Swimming Pond
7 Herb Garden
8 Condenser heat pump
9 Solar panels
10 Roof terrace

LYRIC THEATRE COMPLEX

Hong Kong (HK)

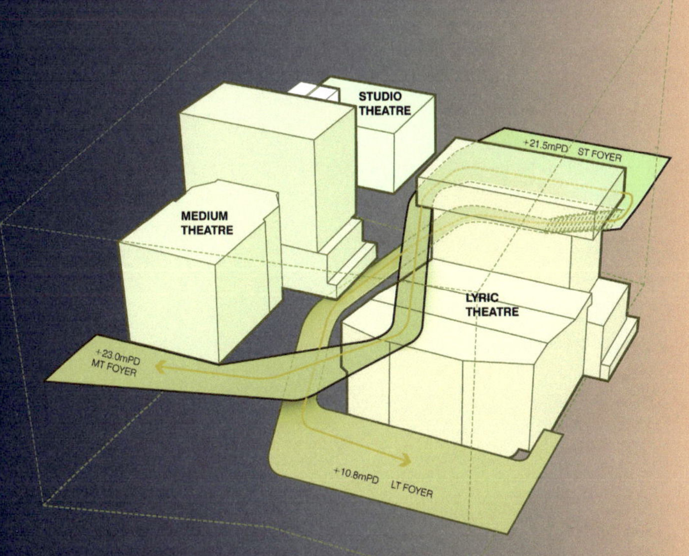
STUDIO
THEATRE
+21.5mPD ST FOYER
MEDIUM
THEATRE
LYRIC
THEATRE
+23.0mPD
MT FOYER
+10.8mPD LT FOYER

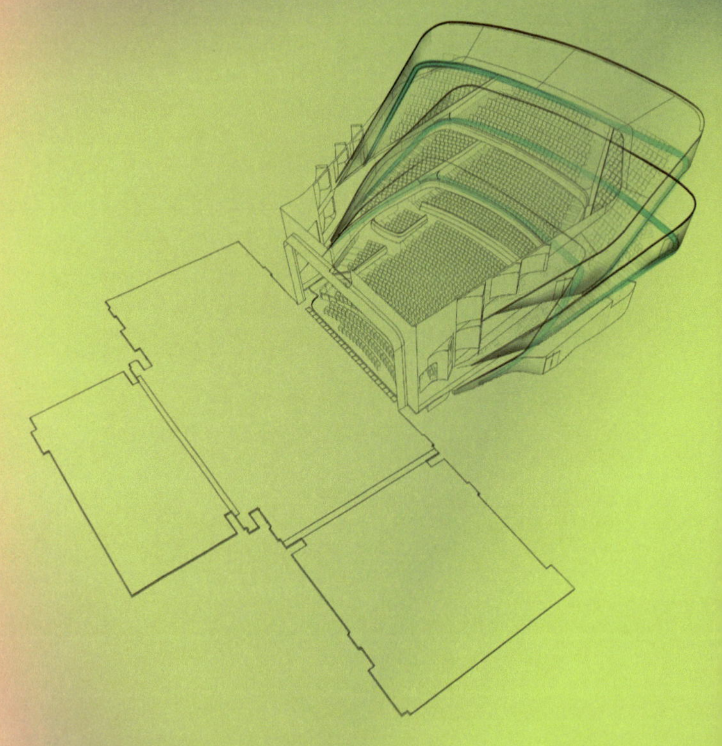

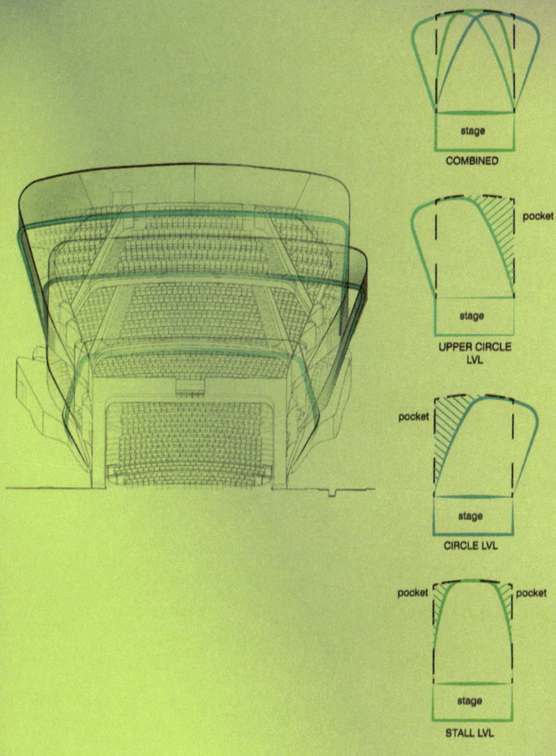
stage
COMBINED
pocket
stage
UPPER CIRCLE LVL
pocket
stage
CIRCLE LVL
pocket
pocket
stage
STALL LVL

PONTE PARODI

Genoa (IT)

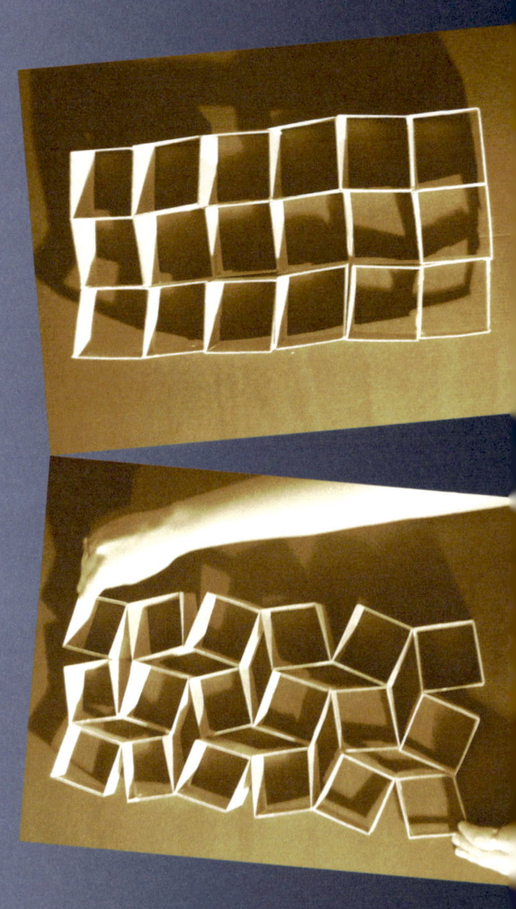

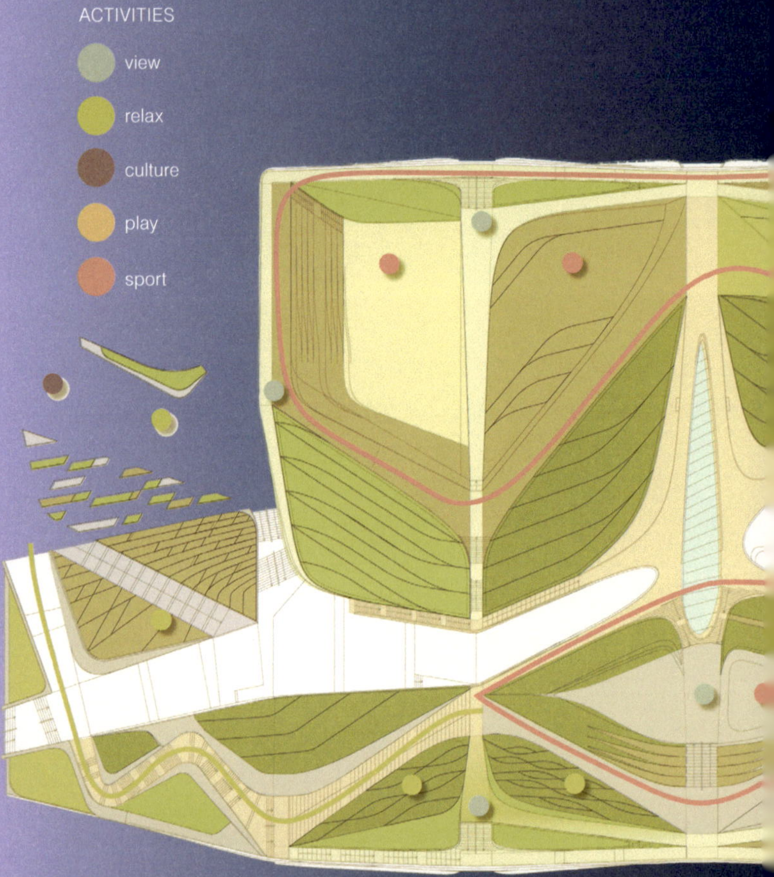
ACTIVITIES
view
relax
culture
play
sport

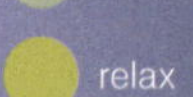

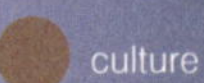

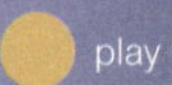

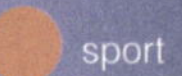

BIG
DETAIL

WASL TOWER

Dubai (AE)

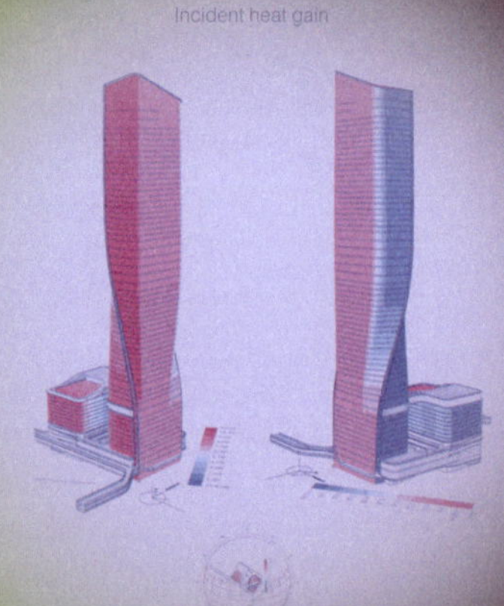

type 1_1/4 of panel width
type 1_2/4 of panel width
type 1_3/4 of panel width
type 1_4/4 of panel width

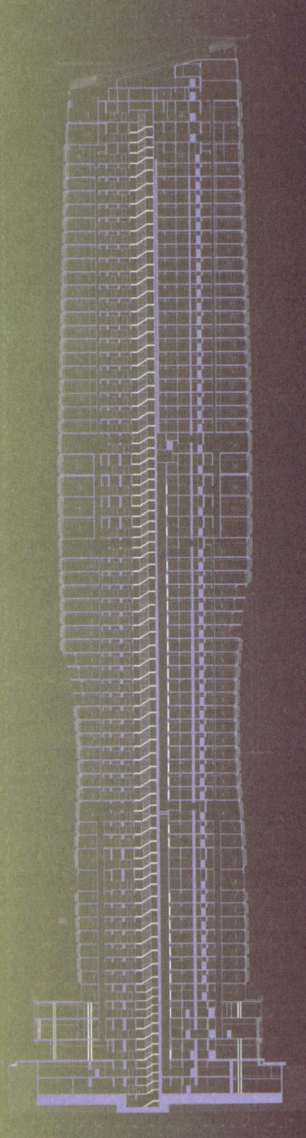

UNIVERSITY OF
BALAMAND
DUBAI

RAFFLES CITY HANGZHOU

Hangzhou (CN)

VIEWS

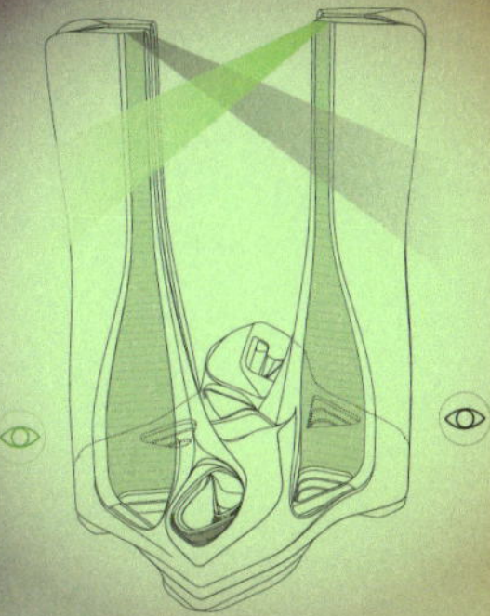

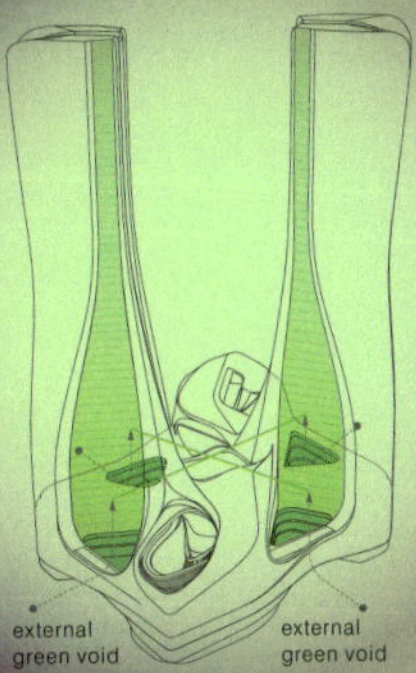
GREEN CONNECTION
external green void
external green void

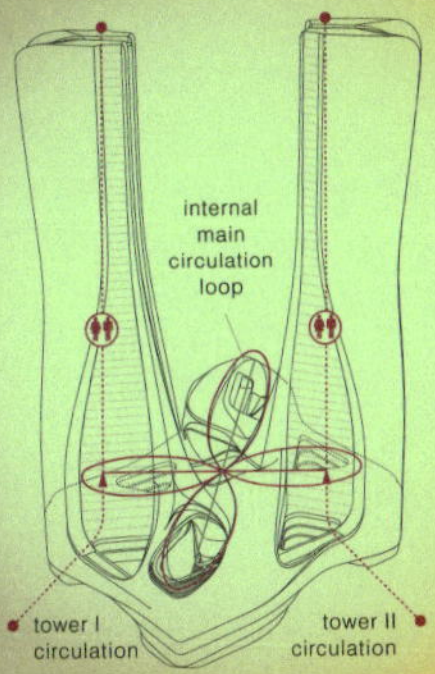
INTERNAL CIRCULATION
internal main circulation loop
tower I circulation
tower II circulation

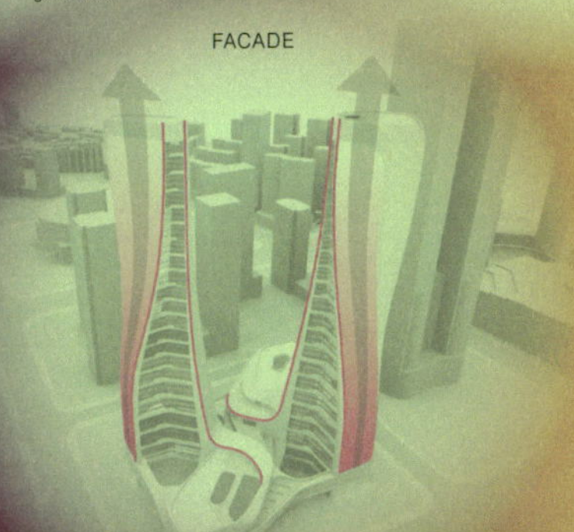
FACADE

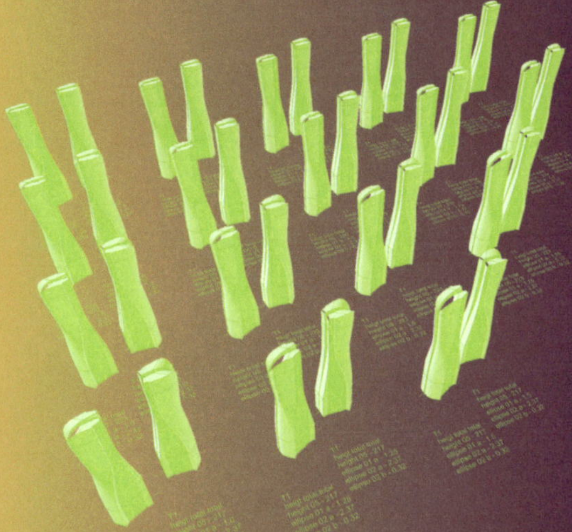

Shading Panel Rotation
100mm
200mm
400mm
600mm
800mm

OPENING SOO
W
W
YOGA
&
Fitness
W

STH BNK BY BEULAH

Melbourne (AU)

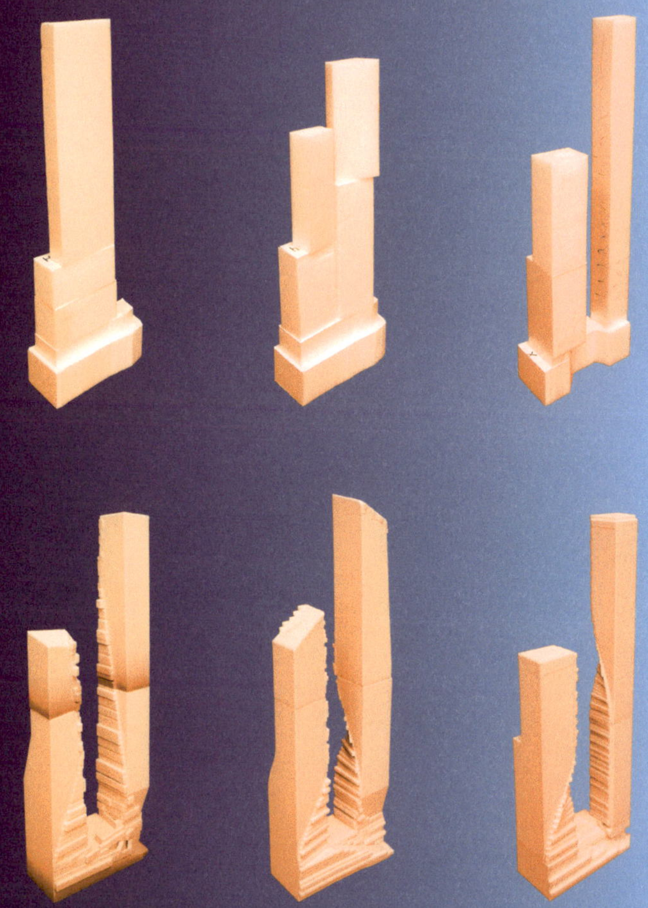

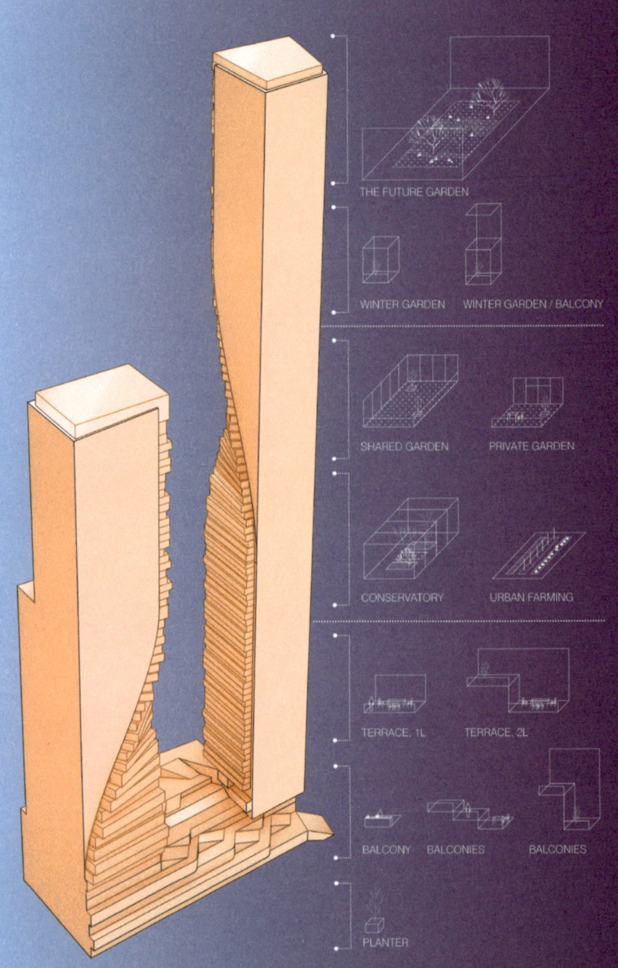
THE FUTURE GARDEN
WINTER GARDEN
WINTER GARDEN / BALCONY
SHARED GARDEN
PRIVATE GARDEN
CONSERVATORY
URBAN FARMING
TERRACE, 1L
TERRACE, 2L
BALCONY
BALCONIES
BALCONIES
PLANTER

ARNHEM CENTRAL STATION TERMINAL

Arnhem (NL)

VILLA NM

Upstate New York (US)

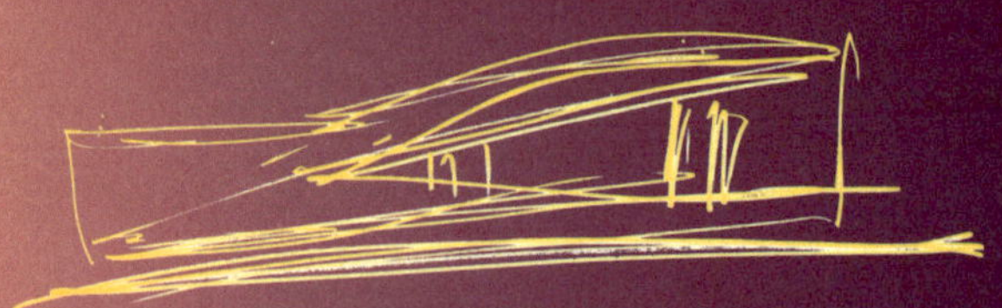

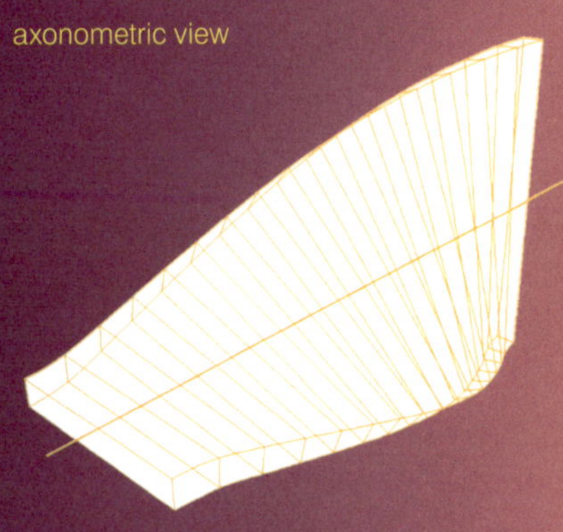
axonometric view

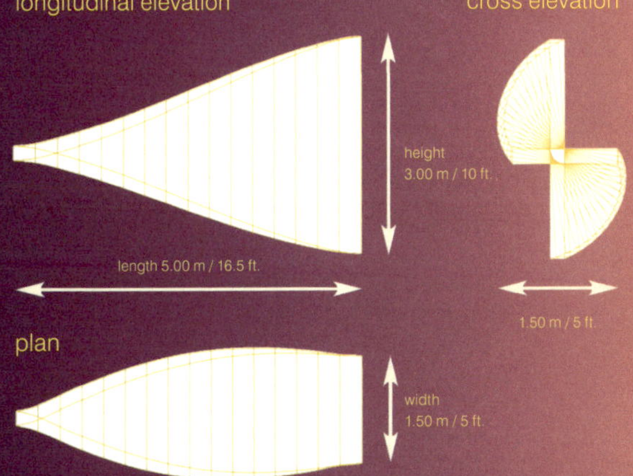
longitudinal elevation
cross elevation
height
3.00 m / 10 ft.
length 5.00 m / 16.5 ft.
1.50 m / 5 ft.
plan
width
1.50 m / 5 ft.

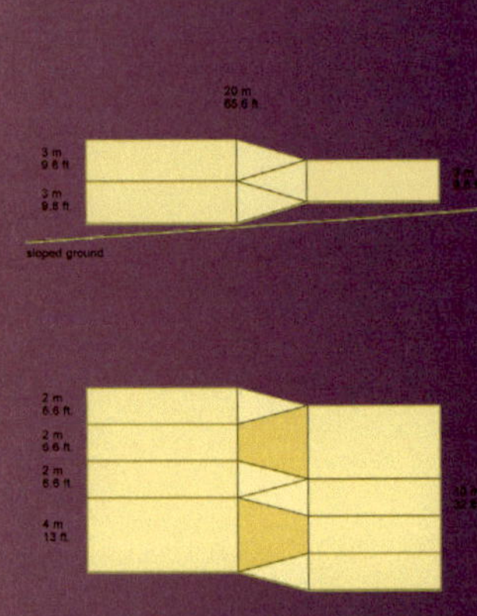
20 m
65.6 ft
3 m
9.8 ft
3 m
9.8 ft
sloped ground
2 m
6.6 ft
2 m
6.6 ft
2 m
6.6 ft
4 m
13 ft
8 m
26 ft
4 m
13 ft
8 m
26 ft

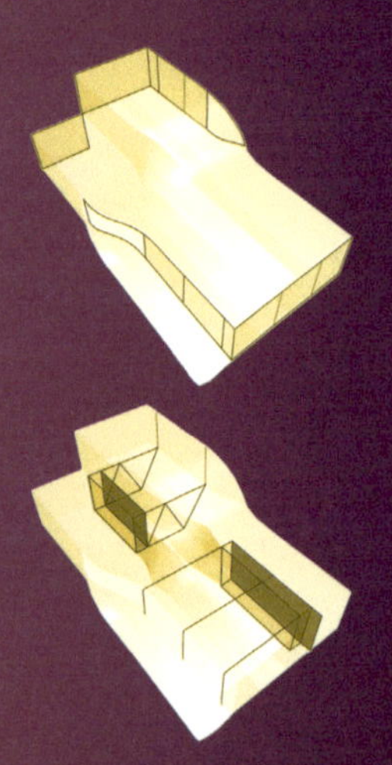

BOOKING.COM URBAN CAMPUS

Amsterdam (NL)

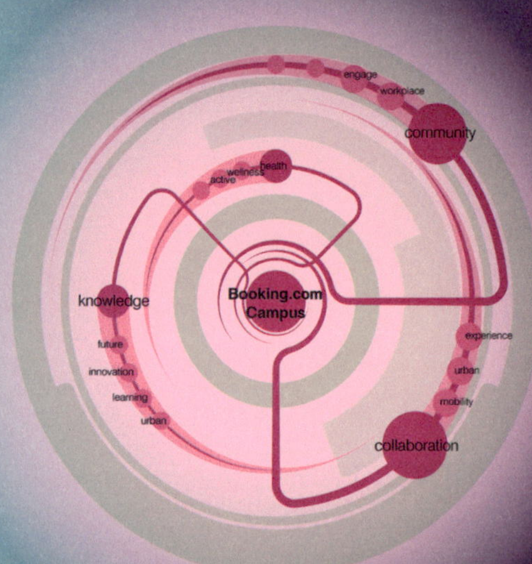

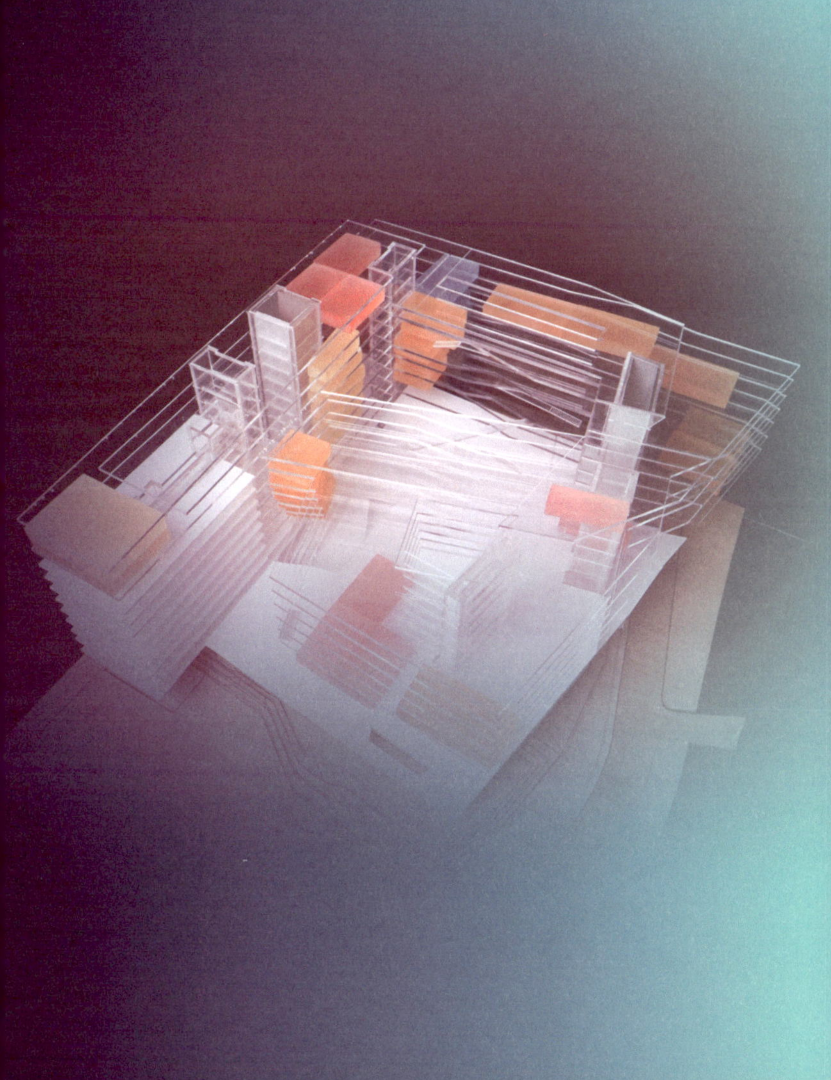

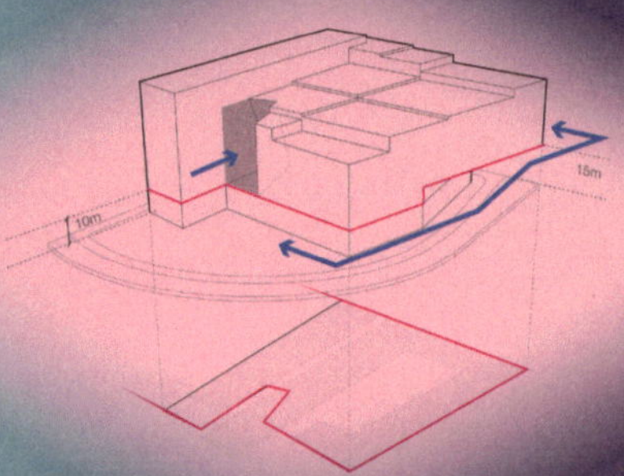

Unifying plots to solidify the whole

Coherent composition of large scale elements

Strong continuity of horizontal

A continuous public interface

Creation of an urban element

A platform for human activity

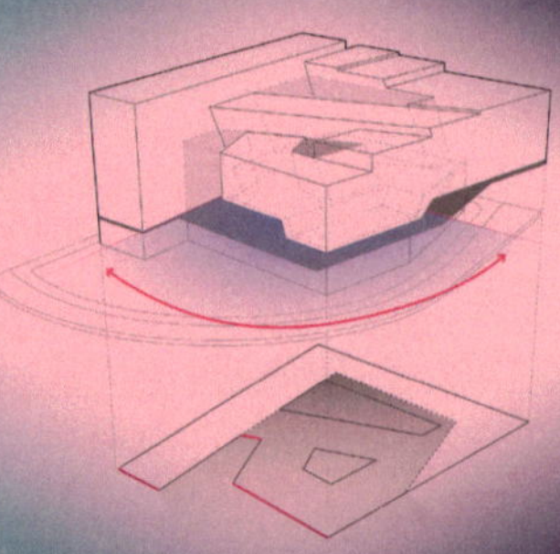

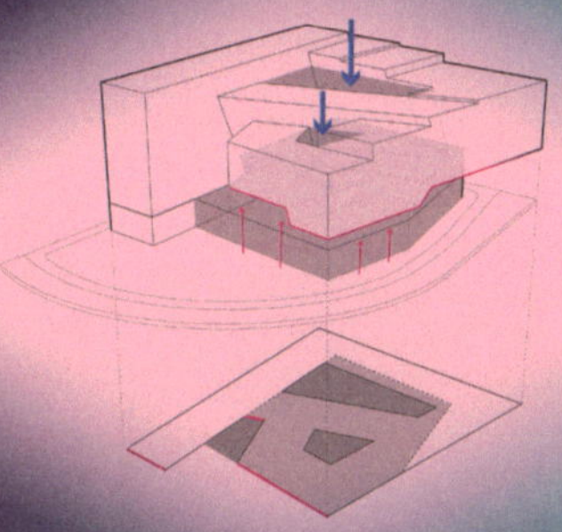

Continuous double height plinth
Sculpting out interior spaces
Lifting building to create maximum public connectivity

A secret landscape
Max out building volume
Utilize terraced roofscape

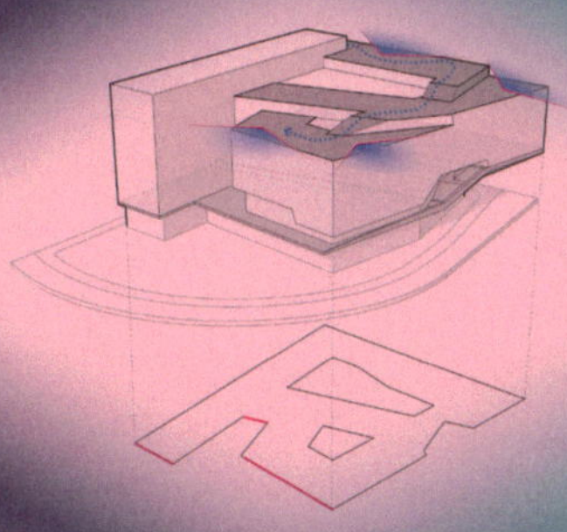

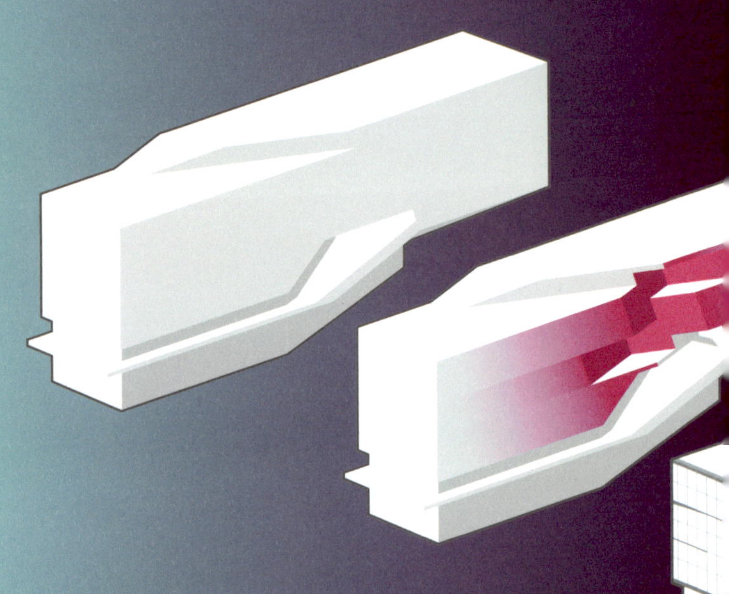

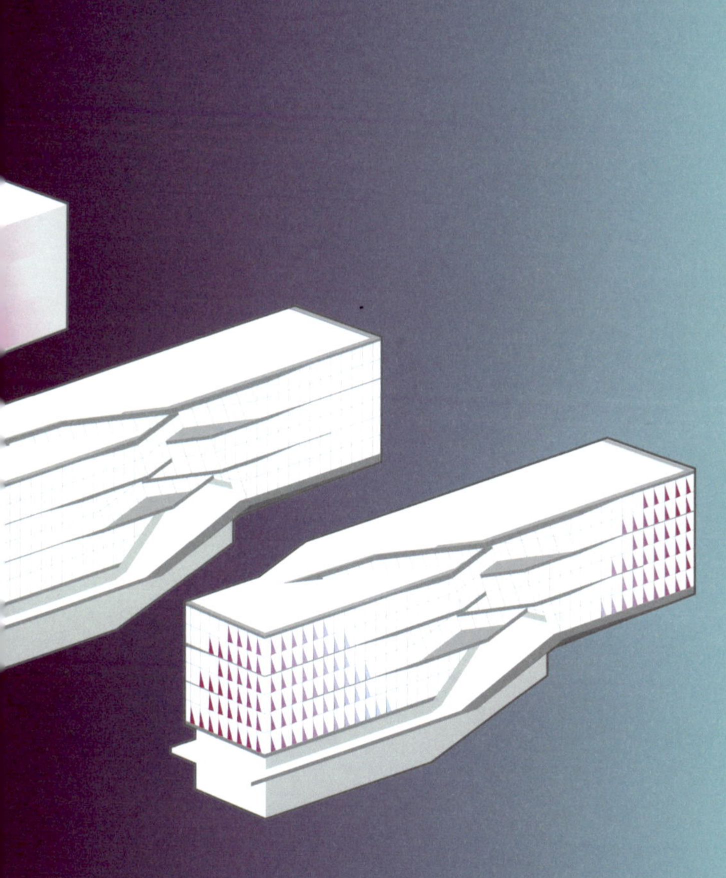

look
mum
no
hands!

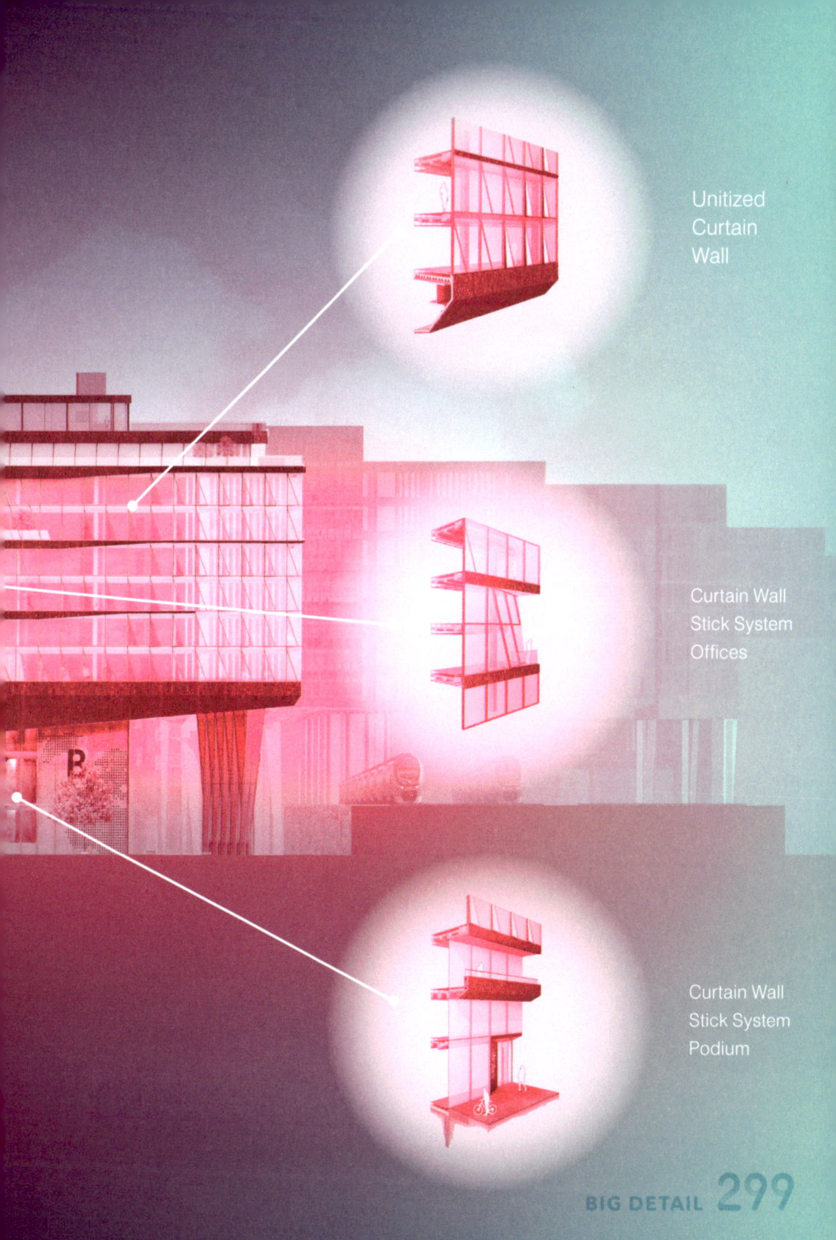
Unitized
Curtain
Wall
Curtain Wall
Stick System
Offices
Curtain Wall
Stick System
Podium

QATAR INTEGRATED RAILWAY

Doha (QA)

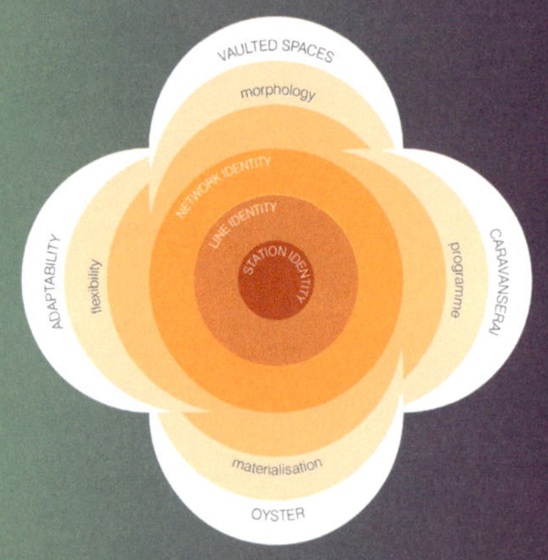

NETWORK IDENTITY

BRAND

LINE IDENTITY

ATMOSPHERE

STATION IDENTITY

CULTURE

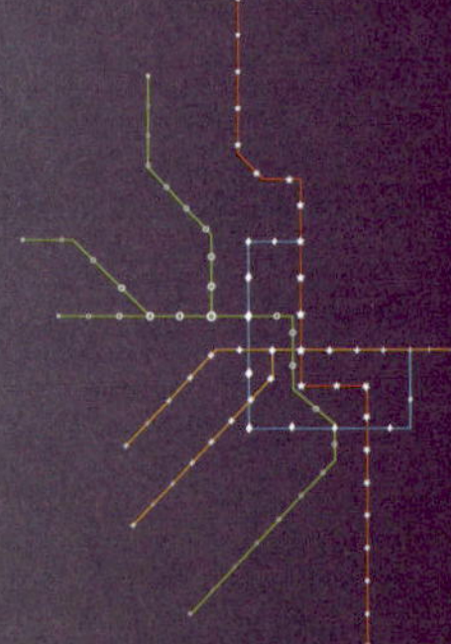

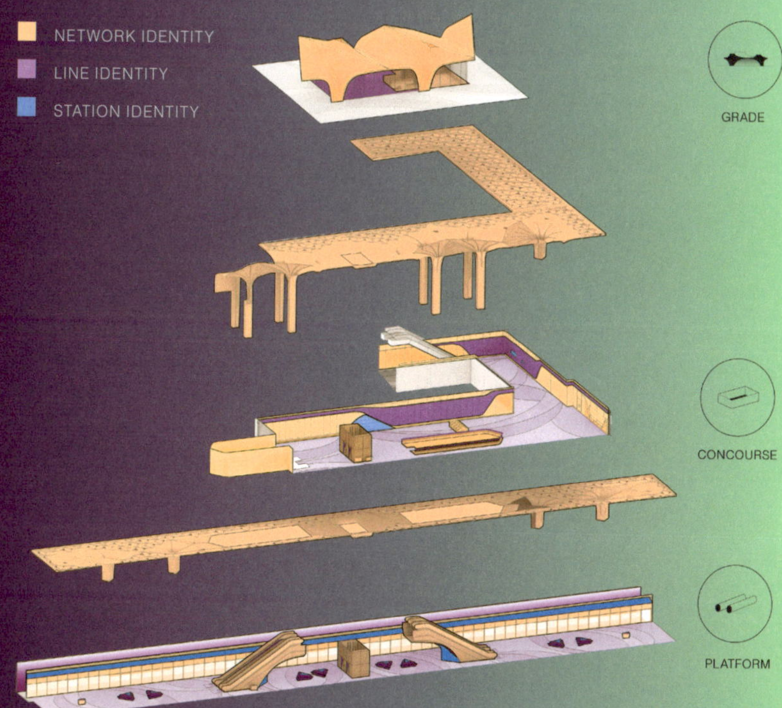

ZONES OF ARCHITECTURAL BRANDING

GRID

COLUMN POSITIONING

SMALL SHELTERS

LARGE SHELTERS

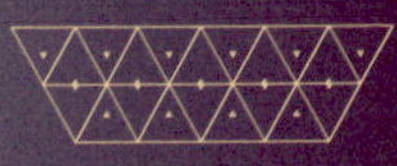

ELEVATED SHELTERS

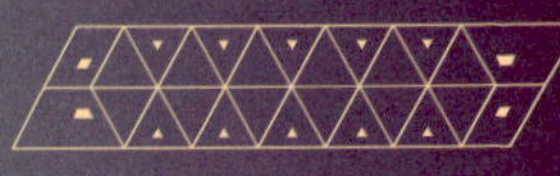

MSHEIREB SHELTERS

SYSTEM

MODULES ASSEMBLING

ENTRANCE FOLDING

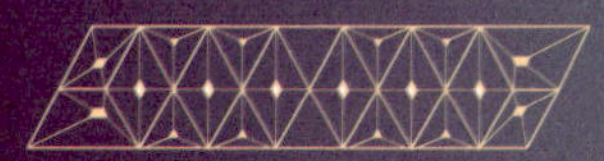

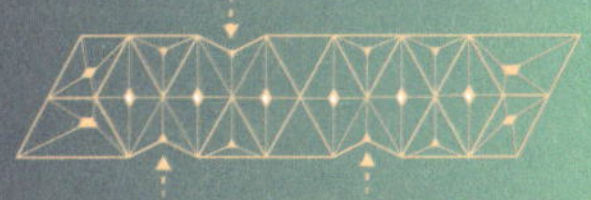

PROJECT CREDITS

ARNHEM CENTRAL STATION (TERMINAL & PARKING GARAGE), ARNHEM, NETHERLANDS, 1996-2015

Public Transport Terminal 1998-2015
UNStudio: Ben van Berkel with Arjan Dingsté and Misja van Veen, René Toet, Marc Hoppermann, Kristoph Nowak, Tobias Wallisser, Nuno Almeida, Rein Werkhoven, Marc Herschel, Sander Versluis, Derrick Diporedjo, Ahmed El-Shafei, Matthew Johnston, Juliane Maier, Daniel Gebreiter, Kirstin Sandner

Parking Garage 1997-2002
UNStudio: Ben van Berkel and Caroline Bos with Sibo de Man, Tobias Wallisser, Jacques van Wijk, Nuno Almeida and Ton van den Berg, Marc Herschel, Matthew Johnston, Paul Vriend, Jacco van Wengerden, Mark Westerhuis, Eli Aschkenasy, Remko van Heumen, Jeroen Tax, Khoi Tran, Marcel Buis, Sander Versluis
Advisors: Masterplan phase: Architect: UNStudio; Structural/Civil Engineering, Transport Planning: Arup. Design and specifications phase: Structural Engineering: Arup (public transport terminal), Van der Werf & Lankhorst (bus station, car park, office square); MEP: Arcadis; Fire safety: DGMR Bouw BV; Public transport terminal lighting: Arup; Public space lighting: Atelier LEK; Wayfinding: Bureau Mijksenaar; Building specifications: ABT; Landscaping design: Bureau B+B stedebouw en landschapsarchitectuur; Project management to Definitive Design: Arcadis. Engineering and construction of pedestrian tunnel: Main contractor: Besix-Welling; Tendering phase contractor: Arcadis. Engineering and construction phase 1: pedestrian tunnel and public transport terminal: Main contractor: construction consortium BAM Ballast Arnhem Centrum VOF (BBB, BAM & Ballast Nedam); Structural engineering, Lighting, Climate and Sustainability: Arup; MEP: BAM Techniek, Unica. Engineering and construction phase 2: public transport terminal: Main contractor: construction consortium OV-Terminal Arnhem (BCOVTA, BAM & Ballast Nedam); Structural engineer: BAM Advies & Engineering, ABT; MEP: BAM Techniek, Unica

MERCEDES-BENZ MUSEUM, STUTTGART, GERMANY, 2001-2006
UNStudio: Ben van Berkel, Tobias Wallisser, Caroline Bos with Marco Hemmerling, Hannes Pfau and Wouter de Jonge, Arjan Dingsté, Götz Peter Feldmann, Björn Rimner, Sebastian Schaeffer, Andreas Bogenschuetz, Uli Horner, Ivonne Schickler, Dennis Ruarus, Erwin Horstmanshof, Derrick Diporedjo, Nanang Santoso, Robert Brixner, Alexander Jung, Matthew Johnston, Rombout Loman, Arjan van der Bliek, Fabian Evers, Nuno Almeida, Ger Gijzen, Tjago Nunes, Boudewijn Rosman, Ergian Alberg, Gregor Kahlau, Mike Herud, Thomas Klein, Simon Streit, Taehoon Oh, Jenny Weiss, Philipp Dury, Carin Lamm, Anna Carlquist, Jan Debelius, Daniel Kalani, Evert Klinkenberg
Advisors: Realisation: UNStudio with Wenzel + Wenzel, Stuttgart; Exhibition Concept and Design: HG Merz, Stuttgart; Interior: UNStudio with Concrete Architectural Associates, Amsterdam; Curtain design: Inside outside - Petra Blaisse, Amsterdam; Structure: Werner Sobek Ingenieure, Stuttgart; Geometry: Arnold Walz, Stuttgart; Climate engineering: Transsolar Energietechnik, Stuttgart; Cost estimation: Nanna Fütterer, Stuttgart/Berlin; Infrastructure: David Johnston, Arup, London; Landscaping: Knoll Ökoplan GmbH, Sindelfingen

LIVING TOMORROW, AMSTERDAM, NETHERLANDS, 2000-2003
UNStudio: Ben van Berkel with Igor Kebel, Aad Krom, Martin Kuitert, Markus Berger, Ron Roos
Advisors: Executive Architect: Bart Thijs

MÖBIUS HOUSE, HET GOOI, NETHERLANDS, 1993-1998
UNStudio: Ben van Berkel with Aad Krom, Jen Alkema and Matthias Blass, Remco Bruggink, Marc Dijkman, Casper le Fevre, Rob Hootsmans, Tycho Soffree, Giovanni Tedesco, Harm Wassink
Advisors: Landscape architect: West 8, Rotterdam; Structural Engineering: ABT, Velp

THE ELLIPSICOON, MANILA, PHILIPPINES, 2015
UNStudio: Ben van Berkel with Ren Yee and Philipp Meise, Peng Wang

THE CHANGING ROOM, VENICE BIENNALE OF ARCHITECTURE, 2008
UNStudio: Ben van Berkel, Caroline Bos with Christian Veddeler and Hans-Peter Nuenning, Steffen Riegas
Advisors: Light design with: Meso Digital Interiors, Frankfurt; Engineering and building: p&p gmbh, Fuerth/Odenwald

CENTRE FOR VIRTUAL ENGINEERING (ZVE), STUTTGART, GERMANY, 2006-2012
UNStudio: Ben van Berkel, Harm Wassink with Florian Heinzelmann, Tobias Wallisser, Marc Herschel, Kristoph Nowak and Christiane Reuther, Aleksandra Apolinarska, Marc Hoppermann, Moritz Reichartz, Norman Hack, Marcin Koltunski, Peter Irmscher
ASPlan: Horst Ermel, Leopold Horinek, Lutz Weber, Stefan Hausladen, Jürgen Bär, Gunawan Bestari, Joachim Deis, Bernd Hasse, Marlene Hertzler, Michael Kapouranis, Vladislav Litz, Thomas Thrun
Advisors: Structural Engineering: BKSI; Mechanical Engineering: Rentschler und Riedesser; Electric Engineering: IB Müller & Bleher; Landscape Architect: Gänssle + Hehr; Accoustics, Energy ENEV, Building Simulation: Brüssau Bauphysik; Fire Safety Advisor: Halfkann + Kirchner; Topographical Survey: Vermessung Hils; Geological Survey: Dr. Alexander Szichta; DGNB: KOP Real Estate Solutions

EDUCATION EXECUTIVE AGENCY AND TAX OFFICES, GRONINGEN, NETHERLANDS, 2006-2011
UNStudio: Ben van Berkel, Caroline Bos, Gerard Loozekoot, with Jacques van Wijk, Frans van Vuure, Lars Nixdorff and Jesca de Vries, Ramon van der Heijden, Alicja Mielcarek, Eric den Eerzamen, Wendy van der Knijff, Machiel Wafelbakker, Timothy Mitanidis, Maud van Hees, Pablo Herrera Paskevicius, Martijn Prins, Natalie Balini, Peter Moerland, Arjan van der Bliek, Alexander Hugo, Gary Freedman, Jack Chen, Remco de Hoog, Willi van Mulken, Yuri Werner, René Rijkers, Machteld Kors, Leon Bloemendaal, Erwin Horstmanshof
Advisors: Interior: Studio Linse; Structure, Installations: Arup; Landscaping: Lodewijk Baljon; Wayfinding: Buro van Baar; Internal Logistics: YNNO; Acoustics: DGMR; Fire Prevention: EFPC; Prefab Structure: Ingenieursbureau Wassenaar; Drawing agency: BTS Bouwkundig Tekenburo Sneek; Maintenance: ISS Nederland B.V; Environmental Technology: Peutz; Ecology: WUR (Wageningen University & Research Centre); Management and Costing: Strukton Bouw en Vastgoed

NMR FACILITY, UTRECHT, NETHERLANDS, 1997-2000
UNStudio: Ben van Berkel with Harm Wassink, Walther Kloet And Marion Regitko, Jacco van Wengerden, Ludo Grooteman, Remco Bruggink, Laura Negrini, Paul Vriend, Mark Westerhuis, Jeroen Kreijnen, Henri Snel, Marc Prins, Aad Krom
Advisors: Constructor: ABT, Velp; Contractor: Nelissen van Egteren, Utrecht and Hoofddorp; Installations: Smits van Burgst, Zoetermeer

THE VALKHOF MUSEUM NIJMEGEN, NETHERLANDS, 1995-1999
UNStudio: Ben van Berkel with Henri Snel and Rob Hootsmans, Remco Bruggink, Jacco van Wengerden, Hugo Beschoor Plug, Marc Dijkman, Florian Fischer, Carsten Kiselowsky, Walther Kloet, Florian Fischer, Carsten Kiselowsky, Luc Veeger
Advisors: Landscape architect: Bureau B&B, Stedenbouw en landschapsarchitectuur, Amsterdam; Technical management: ABT, Velp; Technical consultants: Ketel Raadgevende Ingenieurs, Arnhem; Project management: Berns Projekt Management, Nijmegen

NATIONAL ART MUSEUM OF CHINA (NAMOC), BEIJING, CHINA, 2010
UNStudio: Ben van Berkel, Caroline Bos, Gerard Loozekoot with Joerg Petri, Sander Versluis and Tatjana Gorbatschewskaja, Aurelie Hsiao, Amanda Chan, Imola Berczi, Philip Meise, Tina Kortmann, Hans Kooij, Mo Ching Ying Lai
Advisors: Collaborating Artist: Song Dong; Façade, Structure, MEP, Acoustic: Bollinger & Grohmann, Frankfurt am Main, Germany; Engineering: Bollinger & Grohmann, Frankfurt am Main, Germany

OPPO FLAGSHIP STORE, GUANGZHOU, CHINA, 2019-2020
UNStudio: Ben van Berkel, Hannes Pfau, Garett Hwang with Alexander Meyers, Ana Castaingts Gomez, Piao Liu, Jing Xu, Idil Kantarci, Diego Ramirez Leon, Praneet Verma
Advisors: Local Design Institute: DOP Design; Installation & Exhibition: Leaping Creative; Lighting: brandston partnership inc. (BPI)

UNX2, AMSTERDAM, NETHERLANDS, UNITED NUDE, 2015
UNStudio: Ben van Berkel with Harlen Miller and William de Boer
Advisors: United Nude: Rem D. Koolhaas with Michal Kukucka

MUMUTH MUSIC THEATRE, GRAZ, AUSTRIA, 1998-2008
UNStudio: Ben van Berkel, Caroline Bos with Hannes Pfau and Miklos Deri, Kirsten Hollmann, Markus Berger, Florian Pischetsrieder, Uli Horner, Albert Gnodde, Peter Trummer, Maarten van Tuijl, Matthew Johnston, Mike Green, Monica Pacheco, Ger Gijzen, Wouter de Jonge
Advisors: Engineering: Arup London; Engineering execution: Peter Mandl ZT GmbH; Structural Engineering: Arge Statik, Graz;

Specifications: Housinc Bauconsult GmbH, Vienna; Electrical: Klauss Elektro-Anlagen Planungsgesellschaft m.b.H; Acoustic and Building Physics: ZT Gerhard Tomberger, Graz. Pro Acoustic Engineering Thorsten Rohde, Graz; Technique Stage: e.f.f.e.c.t.s. techn. Büro GmbH, Klosterneuburg; Interior: P + P Holzbau GmbH / vectogramm; Mechanical: Anton Hofstätter GmbH; Electrical: Siemens Bacon GmbH & Co KG; Landscape: Granit Gesellschaft m.b.H.; Landscape design: UNStudio

THEATRE AGORA, LELYSTAD, NETHERLANDS, 2002-2007
UNStudio: Ben van Berkel, Gerard Loozekoot with Jacques van Wijk and Job Mouwen, Holger Hoffmann, Khoi Tran, Christian Veddeler, Christian Bergmann, Sabine Habicht, Ramon Hernandez, Ron Roos, Rene Wysk, Claudia Dorner, Markus Berger, Markus Jacobi, Ken Okonkwo, Jorgen Grahl-Madsen
Advisors: Executive architect: B+M, Den Haag; Theatre technique: Prinssen en Bus Raadgevende Ingenieurs, Uden; Engineering: Pieters Bouwtechniek, Almere; Acoustics/Fire strategy: DGMR, Arnhem

ECHO, TU DELFT, NETHERLANDS, 2017-2022
UNStudio: Ben van Berkel, Arjan Dingsté with Marianthi Tatari, Jaap-Willem Kleijwegt, Ariane Stracke and Piotr Kluszczynski, Thys Schreij, Mitchel Verkuijlen, Bogdan Chipara, Krishna Duddumpudi, Fabio Negozio, Ryan Henriksen, Shangzi Tu, Xinyu Wang, Marian Mihaescu
Advisors: Arup: Structural Engineer, MEP and Building Physics; BBN: Building Cost Consultant; Contractor: BAM Bouw en Techniek; Project Management and Construction Management: Stevens van Dijck

LOUIS VUITTON FLAGSHIP STORE, OSAKA, JAPAN, 2006
UNStudio: Ben van Berkel, Caroline Bos, Astrid Piber with Mirko Bergmann and Sebastian Schott, Ger Gijzen, Cristina Bolis, Juliane Maier, Albert Gnodde, Andreas Brink, Michael Knauss, Morten Krog, Silvan Oesterle, Machteld Kors
Advisors: Arup, Amsterdam: Structure, SMEP; Arup Lighting, Amsterdam: Lighting design; Arup GmbH, Berlin: Façade Engineering

WIEN MITTE URBAN COMPETITION, VIENNA, AUSTRIA, 2003
UNStudio: Ben van Berkel, Caroline Bos, Tobias Wallisser with Markus Hudert, Alicia Velazquez and Michaela Tomaselli, Christina Bolis, Cornelia Faisst, Alice Gramigna, Olaf Gipser, Hannes Pfau, Astrid Piber
Advisors: David Johnston, Arup, London: Infrastructure; Werner Sobek Ingenieure, Stuttgart: Structural Engineering; Pablo Vaggione, Madrid: Feasibility

BURNHAM PAVILION, MILLENNIUM PARK, CHICAGO, USA, 2009
UNStudio: Ben van Berkel, Caroline Bos with Christian Veddeler, Wouter de Jonge and Hans-Peter Nuenning, Ioana Sulea
Advisors: Garofalo Architects: Douglas Garofalo with Grant Gibson; Structural Engineering: Chris Rockey; Light Installation with: Daniel Sauter, Tracey Dear

THE W.I.N.D. HOUSE, NORTH HOLLAND, NETHERLANDS, 2008-2014
UNStudio: Ben van Berkel, Caroline Bos, Astrid Piber with Ger Gijzen, René Wysk and Luis Etchegorry, William de Boer, Elisabeth Brauner, Albert Gnodde, Cheng Gong, Eelco Grootjes, Daniela Hake, Patrik Noome, Kristin Sandner, Beatriz Zorzo Talavera
Advisors: Structural Engineer: Pieters Bouwtechniek, Haarlem; Mechanical, plumbing: Ingenieursburo Linssen bv., Amsterdam; Electrical and Domotica: Elektrokern Solutions, Alkmaar; Building Physics: Mobius Consult, Driebergen; Interior Design: UNStudio, Tim-Alkmaar, Alkmaar; Landscape Design: UNStudio; Lighting Design: Elektrokern Solutions, Alkmaar; Special Acoustics: Hans Koomans Studio Design, Amsterdam; Cost Management: Basalt bouwadvies bv., Nieuwegein, Studio Bouwhaven bv

LYRIC THEATRE COMPLEX, HONG KONG, 2014-2023
UNStudio: Ben van Berkel, Hannes Pfau with Garett Hwang, Shuyan Chan and Sean Ellis, Praneet Verma, Josias Hamid, Irina Bogdan, Alexander Meyers, Jeff Lam, Iker Mugarra Flores, Deepak Jawahar, Mimmo Barbaccia, Evan Shieh, William Benjamin Lucas, Caroline Smith, Vera Kleesattel, Albert Lo, Arnold Wong, Emily Yan, Jan Henao, Haibo He, Abraham Fung, Mihai Soltuz, Betty Fan, Johnny Chan, Berta Sola Sanchez, Eric Jap, Chuanzhong Zhang, Kyle Chou, Bennet Hu, Kenneth Sit, Kevin Yu, Weihong Dong, Stephni Jacobson, Piao Liu, Francois Gandon, James Jones, Mingxuan Xie, Iris Pastor, Jonathan Rodgers, Kaisi Hsu, Pragya Vashisht, Nora Schueler
Lead Consultants: UNStudio / AD+RG
Advisors:
AECOM: Structure, Civil, Geotechnical; WSP: MEP, Environmental; The Space Factory, Carr and Angier: Theatre Consultant; Marshall Day:

Acoustic Consultant; inhabit: Facade Consultant; LWK Partners: Landscape Consultant; a.g Licht: Lighting Consultant; isBIM: BIM Consultant; MVA: Traffic Consultant

PONTE PARODI, GENOA, ITALY, 2001–PRESENT
UNStudio: Ben van Berkel, Caroline Bos, Astrid Piber with Nuno Almeida and (Design Development/Building Permit) Mirko Bergmann, Margherita Del Grosso, Veronica Baraldi, Kristin Sandner, Abhijit Kapade, Chiara Marchionni, Cristina Ferreira, Casper Damkier, Rainer Schmidt, Adrien Leduc, Lorenzo Vianello; (Schematic Design) Cristina Bolis, Paolo Bassetto, Alice Gramigna, Michaela Tomaselli; (Competition) Cristina Bolis, Peter Trummer, Tobias Wallisser, Olga Vazquez-Ruano, Ergian Alberg, Stephan Miller, George Young, Jorge Pereira, Mónica Pacheco, Tanja Koch, Ton van den Berg
Advisors: Structure: d'Appolonia, Genoa; Building Services: Manens, Verona; Traffic: Systematica, Milan; Project Coordination: Studio Augusti, Genoa; (Competition) Infrastructure and Structure: Arup, London; Off-shore Construction: Grootint bv

WASL TOWER, DUBAI, UNITED ARAB EMIRATES, 2014–PRESENT
UNStudio: Ben van Berkel, Gerard Loozekoot, Frans van Vuure with Harlen Miller, Crystal KH Tang, Nick Marks and Megan Hurford, Machiel Wafelbakker, Derrick Diporedjo, Matthew Harrison, Aleksandra Sliwinska, Pietro Scarpa, Mihai Soltuz, Fernando Herrera, Jung Jae Suh, Jae Geun Ahn, Henk van Schuppen, Elizabeth White, Pieter Doets and Dana Behrman, Roman Kristesiashvili, Filippo Lodi, Rene Wysk, Hans Kooij, Nanang Santoso, Thomas van Bekhoven, Ka Shin Lu, Patrik Noome, Philip Wilck, Shankar Ramakrishan, Meng Zhang
Werner Sobek: Contractual Partner, Lead Consultant Engineering
Advisors: Structural Engineering: Werner Sobek, Stuttgart; Facade Engineering: Werner Sobek, Stuttgart; Sustainability: Werner Sobek Green Technologies, Stuttgart; Acoustic Engineering: Werner Sobek Green Technologies, Stuttgart; MEP Engineering: Werner Sobek, London; Local MEP Engineering: Seed, Dubai; Architect of Record: U+A Architects, Dubai; Light Design: Arup, Amsterdam; Landscape Architect: Green4Cities, Vienna; Cost Consultant: Kulkarni Quantity Surveyors, Dubai; FLS Consultant: Aecom, Dubai; Vertical Transportation: Dunbar & Boardman / TÜV SÜD, London; AV/IT Consultant: Shen Milson Wilke; Wind Engineering: Wacker Ingenieure; Kitchen Consultant: Sefton Horn Winch; Pool Engineering: Barr & Wray, Dubai; Interior Design Hotel: GA Design, London UK; Interior Design F&B: AB Concept, Hong Kong

RAFFLES CITY HANGZHOU, CHINA, 2008–2016
UNStudio: Ben van Berkel, Astrid Piber, Hannes Pfau. Project Team: Shu Yan Chan, Markus van Aalderen, Juergen Heinzel, Abhijit Kapade, Tom Minderhout, Marc Salemink, Juliane Maier, Hisa Matsunaga, Garett Hwang, Miklos Deri, Fernie Lai, Praneet Verma, James Leng, Steffen Riegas, Gary Freedman, Shuojiong Zhang; Team Members in different Project Phases (in alphabetical order): Adrian Schmitz, Alexander Hugo, Andreas Bogenschuetz, Anna von Roeder, Bartosz Lamperski, Brendon Carlin, Christian Veddeler, Costa Krautwald, Craig Yan, Cristina Gimenez, Daniel Bazo Hernandez, David Chen, Felix Lohrmann, Florian Heinzelmann, Freek Waltmann, Georg Willheim, Hans-Peter Nuenning, Ioana Sulea, Johan Andersson, Ke Zou, Luming Wang, Magda Smolinska, Marcin Koltunski, Marcin Molik, Marina Bozukova, Michael Sims, Mo Ching Ying Lai, Paula Ibarrondo, Peter Moerland, Qiwei Liang, Qiyuan Ding, Rein Werkhoven, Richard Teeling, Rikjan Scholten, Rodrigo Canizares, Rudi Nieveen, Shi Yang, Shusuke Inoue, Ting Li, Wenzhen Yi, Wing Tang, Yi Cheng Pan, Zhenfei Wang
Interior: Ben van Berkel, Astrid Piber, Hannes Pfau; Project Team: Garett Hwang, Fernie Lai, Hisa Matsunaga, Juergen Heinzel, Lukas Allner, Marc Salemink, Severin Tuerk, Tom Minderhoud, Abhijit Kapade; Team Members in different Project Phases (in alphabetical order): Craig Yan, Cristina Gimenez, Eric Zhu, Fahad Mohammad, Justin Cheng, Qiyuan Ding, Yang Shi, Yue Zhou
Advisors: Local Design Institute: China United Engineering Corporation, Hangzhou; Structure, Mechanical Engineering, Fire Engineering, LEED: Arup Shanghai, Arup LEED Hong Kong; Traffic Consultant: MVA Transport Consultants; Facade Consultant: Meinhardt Façade Technology (Shanghai) Ltd; Overseas Lighting Consultant: a.g Licht, Bonn; Local Lighting Consultant: LEOX Design Partnership, Shanghai; Landscape Consultant: TOPO Design Group. LLC, Shanghai; Quantity Surveyor: Davis Langdon & Seah Consultancy, Shanghai; MEP Consultant (interior): SAIYO, Shanghai

STH BNK BY BEULAH, MELBOURNE, AUSTRALIA, 2018
UNStudio: Ben van Berkel, Caroline Bos with Jan Schellhoff, Sander Versluis, Milena Stopic and Julia Gottstein, Marco Cimenti, Leon Hansmann,

Perrine Planche, Olga Kovrikova, Carleigh Shannon
Cox Architecture: Phil Rowe, Pete Sullivan, Ian Sutter, Eliza Suffren, Michael Murdock, Noushin Atrvash, William Cassell, Rebekah Collins, Tommy Miller, Alex Leiva
Advisors: Future City, London: Cultural Placemaking; Studio Drift, Amsterdam: Lead Artist; Atelier Ten, Melbourne: Sustainability & Well-being; Grant Associates: Landscape Architects; GTA Consultants: Traffic & Accessibility; Arup, Melbourne: Engineering

VILLA NM, UPSTATE NEW YORK, USA, 2000-2007
UNStudio: Ben van Berkel with Olaf Gipser and Andrew Benn, Colette Parras, Jacco van Wengerden, Maria Eugenia Diaz, Jan Debelius, Martin Kuitert, Pablo Rica, Olga Vazquez-Ruano
Advisors: Project Consultant: Roemer Pierik, Rotterdam, The Netherlands; Landscape Architect: Nicholas Pouder, ASLA, Pouder Design Group, Patterson NY; Grounds landscaping: Jason Maciejevski, Maciejevski Landscaping, Damascus, PA

BOOKING.COM URBAN CAMPUS, AMSTERDAM, NETHERLANDS, 2015
UNStudio: Ben van Berkel with Arjan Dingsté, Marianthi Tatari, Marc Hoppermann, Misja van Veen, Juergen Heinzel, Ariane Stracke, René Toet and Albert Gnodde, Albert Laarman, Anna Garazdowska, Ardit Curraj, Ayax Abreu, Bruno Peris, Clare Porter, Cristina Bolis, Ergin Birinci, Georgios Siokas, Guilherme Miranda, Ivo van Capelleveen, Izak Kljakovic, Jolien Bruin, Juan Luis Mayen Moran, Ka Shin Liu, Luke Tan, Mahmoud Meligy, Mark Maas, Martin Zangerl, Maya Christodoulaki, Menida Avram, Mitchel Verkuijlen, Olivier Yebra, Pieter Doets, Robbie Neijzen, Ryszard Rychlicki, Alex Tahinos, Argyrios Delithanasis, Bart Bonenkamp, Gary Polk, Ke Quan, Kyle Tousant, Mahmoud Meligy, Ryan Henriksen, Xinyu Wang, Yan Ma. **Model:** Patrik Noome. **Interior fit-out - auditorium, bike entrance and parking, open-air Campus (balconies and rooftop):** Ben van Berkel with Arjan Dingsté, Marianthi Tatari, Ariane Stracke and Antoine van Erp, Cristina Bolis, Yiming Zhang, Mitchel Verkuijlen, Lachlan Million, Lieneke van Hoek
Advisors (DD and TD Stages): a.g Licht: Lighting Design Consultant; Aronsohn: Structural Engineer; B+MBIM Manager; DPA: Building Physics, Acoustic and Fire Life Safety Consultant; IBS: Facade Consultant; IGG: Cost and Quantity Surveying; Techniplan: MEP and Vertical Transportation Consultant. **(TD and CD Stages)**: ICO: MEP Contractor ("Installatie Combinatie ODE"); Kone: Vertical Transportation Contractor; Manntech: Facade access Contractor; Scheldebouw: Facade Contractor; Sorba: Architectural cladding Contractor; Zublin Nederland: Contractor. **Interior fit-out**: Enbiun: F&B Consultant; Heuvelman Sound & Vision: AV Consultant; RHDHV: Acoustic Consultant; Moss: Green Specialist; Studio Rublek: Lighting Design

QATAR INTEGRATED RAILWAY, DOHA, QATAR, 2012-2019
UNStudio: Ben van Berkel, Astrid Piber with Nuno Almeida, Arjan Dingsté and René Rijkers, Marianthi Tatari, Juergen Heinzel, Rob Henderson, Jaap-Willem Kleijwegt, Tom Minderhoud and Wael Batal, Thomas van Bekhoven, Ergin Birinci, William de Boer, Sean Buttigieg, Rodrigo Cañizares, Eric Caspers, Konstantinos Chrysos, Leonhard Clemens, Bas Cuppen, Gokcen Dadas, Eric Eelman, Maurits Fennis, Giacomo Garziano, Ger Gijzen, Albert Gnodde, Ricardo Guedes, Maud van Hees, Maarten Heinis, Lars van Hoften, Marc Hoppermann, Sebastian Janusz, Nemanja Kordić, Dennis Krassenburg, Samuel Liew, Guomin Lin, Chiara Marchionni, Alberto Martinez, Gerben Modderman, Martin Neumann, Patrik Noome, Kristoph Nowak, Maurizio Papa, Bruno Peris, Marcos Polydorou, Clare Porter, Attilio Ranieri, Stefano Rocchetti, Thys Schreij, Georgios Siokas, Ariane Stracke, Luke Tan, Yi-Ju Tseng, Menno Trautwein, Gerasimos Vamvakidis, Laertis Vassiliou, Sander Versluis, Philip Wilck, JooYoun Yoon, Martin Zangerl, Shuang Zhang, Meng Zhao, Jennifer Zitner, Seyavash Zohoori
Advisors: Structure, MEP: RHDHV; Facade engineering: Inhabit; Lighting engineering: a.g Licht; Wayfinding: Mijksenaar; Passenger flow analysis: MIC - Mobility in Chain; Fire and life safety: AECOM